Skills

for
Personal
Historians

*102 Savvy Ideas
to Boost Your Expertise*

DAN CURTIS

Personal History Press

ISBN 978-0-9820134-1-0 (Paperback)

ISBN 978-0-9820134-2-7 (Kindle edition)

ISBN 978-0-9820134-3-4 (Nook edition)

Edited by Kathleen McGreevy

Cover and Interior Design & Layout by Monica Lee

For my mother, Marge Curtis,
and my partner, Jim Osborne

Contents

Foreword

DAN CURTIS STARTED HIS blog about doing personal histories in 2008, when there wasn't much on the Internet about helping people tell their life stories. The Association of Personal Historians (APH) hadn't yet geared itself to offering the range of workshops and courses it now offers and Dan decided that was where he wanted to put his energy.

"When I started it seemed to me it would be a good idea to have a blog as part of my overall marketing and web presence," says Dan. "I knew that if I was to succeed, I had to produce a blog that was relevant, timely, consistent, and readable." He spent months researching what goes into a blog that attracts readers until finally "I decided that I'd better stop with the research and actually 'do it.' At first my blog was directed to the do-it-yourself market of family writers. But I soon became aware that it was difficult to write material that was going to keep these people coming back for more. That's when I decided to write specifically for professional personal historians. No one else was doing it. When I started I had no idea where it would all lead. But I enjoyed the writing and the creativity of finding topics every week to write about."

Buried in Dan's DNA, he writes, is the need to "serve," which is one reason he became a personal historian. It also comes through in the generosity with which he shares the secrets of his craft and trade—most particularly his many posts on how to interview. It is worth buying this book for the suggested interview questions alone, starting with "The Fifty Best Life Story Questions." Equally helpful is his advice on how to interview—how to both listen and look, and how to ask questions that will unlock life stories.

A particular strength of Dan's book is advice about how to work with people who are dying. In 2005, Dan became a volunteer at Victoria Hospice and in 2008 he started a Life Stories program there. This gave him insight into one of the most delicate, difficult, and important types of personal history work possible: helping those who are dying leave a story or a message (or both) for their friends and family. With little time available for interviewing those hospice patients, Dan developed skill in eliciting useful material with questions that go to the core of a person's life. He has trained eleven volunteers to work with dying patients and is still busy managing the program and mentoring the volunteers. He is also writing a manual for other hospices on how to set up and run a similar program.

In June 2013, five years after launching his blog, Dan stopped writing it and turned his energies more toward the hospice work and strong personal interests, such as photography and writing haiku. A year later he decided to "turn out the lights." This was disappointing to his 400 subscribers, many of whom had bookmarked and linked to his blog entries! Luckily Dan's need to serve made this book possible. Now everyone who buys it can easily find material on interviewing, on audio- and video-recording interviews, on preserving digital media, on writing, editing, and publishing a personal history, on leading workshops, on creating an ethical will, on working with clients at the end of life, and on doing it yourself (after all, we personal historians should also be telling our own life stories). You will also find dozens of wonderful—often inspirational—quotations and stories about life story writing and personal history work. And Dan has directed that proceeds from the book go to support the ongoing professional development of members of the APH.

Enjoy what follows—and learn! And thank you, Dan.

—Pat McNees
Past President of the Association of Personal Historians and
Co-Editor of *My Words Are Gonna Linger: The Art of Personal History*

Editor's Preface

IT'S BEEN MY HONOR to help Dan edit and assemble his blog posts into an ebook and book. Over the years that he published the blog, I saved and printed many of his articles. His advice was always practical and insightful, but now that I've had the experience of reading through all the topics at one time, I'm most grateful for his consistent underlying message: saving personal histories is very important work and worthy of our best efforts.

—Kathleen McGreevy
Chapter Savers

Introduction

FOR FIVE YEARS I WROTE a professional blog for personal historians. When I began I had no idea how long it would last or that one day it would be turned into a book. I'm delighted that most of my work has now been saved and will continue to provide support to personal historians for many years to come.

This book isn't a "how to" manual. It isn't meant to be read from cover to cover. Think of it as a buffet of tasty tips rather than a four course meal. Bon appetit!

I'm pleased that all the proceeds from the sale of this book will go to support the ongoing professional development of members of the Association of Personal Historians.

CHAPTER 1:

Interviewing: Basics

1 The #1 Secret to a Successful Life Story Interview

Picture this. You sit down to conduct a personal history interview. You pull out your voice recorder and your client looks stricken. You reassure her that there's no need to worry and ask your first question. She looks at the floor and gives a brief two or three word response. It doesn't get any better. It feels as though you are "pulling teeth." Beads of perspiration break out on your forehead. You finish the interview and leave for home, tired and discouraged.

What went wrong?

Some of you will say it was the voice recorder that made the client uneasy. Nope! Not the recorder. Today's devices are small and unobtrusive. There might be some initial discomfort but it passes—like gas. I've done hundreds of hours of interviews and within a few minutes people forget there's even a recorder in the room. So don't blame the recorder.

Sorry to say but the problem rests with the interviewer. If you're not comfortable with the equipment or are anxious about getting a good interview or are worried about the questions you're going to ask, then your anxiety is going to rub off on your client. Neuroscience research has uncovered "mirror neurons" which seems to indicate that if we see someone frowning or smiling, it triggers a similar internal reaction in us.

In a word, the #1 secret to a successful interview is rapport. Here's what you need to do.

Before the interview, make your initial visit a "get-to-know."

Nothing creates more anxiety in a client than rushing in all "business-like," ready to record. Take an hour to have a conversation with your client. Stress the personal. Imagine you're dropping in on a favorite aunt or uncle. Do talk about the upcoming interview but spend as much time if not more on small talk.

I try to get a quick sense of people's interests by looking at how they've decorated and what treasures they've chosen to display. A question about a painting, photo, or figurine can unlock some charming stories. And it puts your client at ease. Find something in common—maybe it's grandchildren, a favorite author, or similar childhood roots.

Arrive for the interview rested, mindful, focused, and calm.

Remember that clients will pick up on your anxiety. This in turn makes them anxious. When you walk through the door to a client's home, you want to be smiling and aware of what is happening from moment to moment. To do that effectively, you need to be rested and focused solely on the interview at hand. How does your client look? How are you feeling? What extraneous activities or sounds are intruding on your interview space?

Before the interview begins, start with some small talk.

I never set up my recorder or camera for an interview without first engaging my client in some small talk. It can be about the weather, their day or week's activities, or any other subject that's informal. I find a sense of humor and some laughter go a long way to defuse anxiety. I'm also mindful that we've a job at hand and I don't let the chatting eat up too much time.

Set up the recording equipment with practiced nonchalance.

Don't make setting up your recording equipment a "big production." The more I consciously avoid flailing about with my recorder and microphone, the less distressing it is for my client. This means you have to know your equipment superbly. It's not the time to begin fretting over what folder you're recording in or why you're not getting sound in your headphones. It also helps to keep some chit-chat going while you clip on a lavaliere mic and adjust the sound levels.

Rapport. That's the secret.

2 5 Good Reasons to Ditch the Laptop and Handwritten Notes

There's been some discussion among my colleagues at the Association of Personal Historians about the way to record life story interviews. Some personal historians use a digital voice recorder. Others prefer taking notes by hand or typing the interview directly into their laptop.

The latter make it clear they can type as fast as people talk, edit on the fly, maintain eye contact, and save the time and costs of transcribing the interview. For those who take notes by hand, they explain that this helps them keep the story to the essentials. They may record the interview for reference to ensure the accuracy of quotes. All point out that this method of interviewing is what they're comfortable with and their clients are happy with their work.

But achieving the best interview possible has nothing to do with the time and cost of transcriptions, what process a personal historian is most comfortable with, or editing on the fly. These are all factors that speak to the preferences of the personal historian—not the quality of the interview.

1. An integral and invaluable part of any personal history is recording and preserving the spoken word.

Hearing a loved one's voice is a precious remembrance for bereaved families and future generations. Personal histories involve more than assembling edited transcripts into a story.

2. Laptops and note taking are distracting.

I know this from having been interviewed a number of times by journalists. Imagine for a moment that you're talking to a columnist. You're pouring your heart out but she's writing nothing down. Then you move on to something that seems insignificant and the writer starts scribbling furiously. You wonder why these comments elicited such a response. It's unnerving. It'll be unnerving for your clients too.

3. Multitasking doesn't work.

There is now sufficient research to show that the mind can't process more than one thing at a time. People can't type or take notes and be fully engaged with a client at the same time. Trust me. It can't be done.

4. Editing decisions are best made after (not during) an interview.

It's not possible to tell what portions of a narrative need to be dropped until you have a feel for the whole story. An item that seems of little importance at the time of the interview may turn out to be a crucial element in the story.

5. Listening to your interviews improves your skills.

There's tremendous value in recording an interview and being able to play it back. I do it all the time. For one thing, it enables you to see what follow-up questions to ask. But equally important, it gives you an opportunity to assess your strengths and weaknesses as an interviewer.

Conclusion

Not all approaches are equal when it comes to recording personal histories. Choose a good digital recorder and microphone over a laptop or handwritten notes. Your clients will thank you.

3 Are You Creating a Supportive Milieu for Your Personal History Interviews?

You can be a first class interviewer, but if you don't ensure a good interview environment, your chances of getting the best from your client are minimized. Here are four things you can do to create a supportive milieu.

1. Choose a room with lots of "padding."

This is particularly important if you're producing audio or video personal histories. Audio sounds terrible when it's recorded in a room that's all hard surfaces. Stay away from kitchens! Living rooms usually work well because they are filled with drapes, rugs, and upholstered furniture. Try this sound expert's trick. Clap your hands and if you don't hear any reverberation, the space is good for your recording.

2. Find a "best" time for your client.

You want to interview your clients at a time that works for them. Some are morning people and are most animated and alert in the morning. Others find evening a time when they're open to reflection. For others a busy weekly schedule may mean weekends work the best. Be flexible and ensure that you arrange a time that fits your clients' needs rather than your own.

3. Avoid an audience.

You don't want people sitting in on your interview. Ban wives, husbands, kids, friends, long lost relatives, and the neighbor next door. Be firm! Having someone present during your interview is very distracting for both you and your client.

4. Turn off everything that hums, whirs, ticks, or rings.

Picture this. You're leading up to very dramatic, emotional point in your interview when suddenly the telephone rings. Kiss that moment goodbye. No matter how hard you try to recapture it, you'll never get that special moment back. Unplug the telephones. Turn off the refrigerator. Stop the air conditioner or furnace. Silence loud ticking clocks. Just remember to turn everything back on before you leave!

4 4 Action Steps to a Good Life Story Interview

Conducting a good life story interview is a mix of research, talent, training and a little luck. But you can improve your odds. I've been interviewing people for over twenty-five years and I still follow this four point pre-interview plan.

1. Review your previous interview.

Always sit down after an interview and listen to it. Make a list of possible follow-up questions and look at where there's room for improvement.

Maybe you're using a lot of "Uh-huhs" or interrupting frequently. Whatever it is, make a note to change your "bad" interview habits.

2. Prepare your questions.

It's helpful to have a road map of where you want to take the interview. Making up your questions beforehand will give you confidence. You don't need to slavishly follow your list of questions during the interview but knowing you have them is reassuring.

3. Check your equipment.

You don't want to arrive for your interview and discover your audio recorder or microphone battery is dead. As a rule, always carry an extra supply of batteries for emergencies. If you're using a video camera make certain that your camera battery is fully charged and that you have sufficient flash drives. Have extra lamps for any lights you may use. Don't forget to record a test segment on your audio recorder or camcorder to make sure they're working.

4. Avoid rushing.

It's useful not to arrive for your interview in a "frazzle". Make sure you know the route to your subject's home and how long it will take you to get there. This is particularly important for your first visit. I find MapQuest or Google Maps great for showing the best way to get from point A to point B. Leave plenty of time to make your trip.

Also, the day of the interview, make sure that you don't fill up your calendar with multiple appointments or tasks to do before or after the scheduled interview. You don't want to be exhausted before you arrive.

And you don't want to be looking at your watch during the interview, afraid that you might be late for your next appointment.

5 Have You Ever Found Yourself in This Embarrassing Situation?

Here's my story. I remember arriving at a client's home for an interview with my camcorder, tapes, tripod, lights, and...no microphones! Luckily I was only a 10-minute drive from home. I rushed back to retrieve the missing mics and the interview went on. But I was embarrassed. It didn't look professional.

No matter how experienced we are, without a checklist in hand we can sometimes forget an important detail. When I train new life story interviewers for Victoria Hospice, I hand them out a list similar to the one below. You might find it useful. Go ahead and modify it to suit your own needs.

1. At home before leaving for the interview

- Listen to your previous interview – check audio quality, make notes on topics covered, and prepare follow-up questions.
- Prepare interview questions keeping in mind the need for "stories" and "significant" moments.
- Check battery level in recorder.
- Check that the mic is working.
- Check that you have extra recorder and mic batteries.

- Check that you have your headphones and mic packed with your recorder.

- Make sure you've got sufficient gas in your car.

2. At interview location before starting to record

- Make certain all radios, music systems, TVs, and telephones are turned off.

- If other family members or friends are in the room, politely ask them to leave.

- Check on the amount of time you have with your narrator.

- Make sure that your narrator is comfortable and has a glass of water nearby.

- Check to make sure you have a clear view of a timepiece to note the passage of time.

3. During the interview

- Make sure to wear headphones and check that you're hearing audio.

- At the outset of your recording, state the day, month, and year, your name, your narrator's name, and location. Repeat this for each session.

- If you're using only one mic, speak clearly and project your voice toward the narrator's mic so that your voice will be heard on the recording.

- When using a clip-on mic monitor the audio for any interference caused by the narrator's movement.

SKILLS FOR PERSONAL HISTORIANS

- Stop the recording and make the necessary adjustments if the audio is compromised.

- Check the recorder from time to time to monitor the battery level— if low, change batteries immediately.

- Check the clock to make sure you don't go beyond the set time.

- Monitor your narrator's energy level and stop if the person is becoming tired.

4. After the interview

- Remove mic from recorder and turn it OFF.

- Do not remove batteries from the mic or the recorder.

- Turn narrator's telephone and appliances back on.

- Check to make sure you've left nothing behind.

- Arrange with your narrator a date and time for the next interview.

6 How to Get the Stories in a Life Story Interview

What makes a great story? If you think of the characteristics of your favorite novels, you'll probably come up with a list like mine:

- engaging characters

- interesting settings

- intriguing and coherent plot

- surprising twists and turns

- conflict and resolution

These same story elements also apply to non-fiction works like life stories or memoirs. Inexperienced personal historians sometimes forget this. Great stories engage the reader or listener.

A narrative that reads, "This happened and then that happened. And then this happened followed by that happening" is not engaging. It's simply a recitation of events, places, and details. It's boring.

Here's how you can ensure that you get great stories:

As you interview a client, listen carefully and ask yourself the following questions:

- Does the story have a strong sense of place?
- Are the characters well drawn?
- Is the story intriguing?
- Am I drawn in?
- Am I delighted?
- Am I surprised?
- Is there a sense of moving forward—a journey?
- Is the storyteller emotionally connected to the story?
- Is this a crucial story in the person's life? Is it a turning point?
- Does the story seem to have a purpose? That is, is it worth telling?

If your answer is "No" to any one of these, gently redirect the interview. Ask questions that will turn the "No's" into "Yes's."

You'll be surprised at how much more engaging your client's stories will be. Guaranteed.

13

7 9 Secrets of a Good Interview

If you decide to produce a personal history of someone in your family, here are some useful tips to keep in mind.

1. Get the best recorder and lavaliere (clip-on) microphone you can afford.

No matter how good your interview, it will be ruined if the quality of the recording is poor. Avoid mics that are built-in the recorder. And if possible, use a headphone so that you can hear if you're capturing the sound you need.

2. Avoid having other people in the same room.

This can make your subject nervous and distracted. It could make you tense as well.

3. Make certain there isn't any background noise.

The playing of radios, stereos, or TVs or the sound of people cleaning the house or washing dishes can be very distracting. And if you intend to edit and transfer the interview to a CD or audiotape as a gift, you don't want it ruined by all kinds of "racket" going on in the background.

4. Relax your subject.

Most people feel a little nervous when they start to be interviewed. Begin with some "small talk" about the weather or a favorite pastime. Make sure your subject is sitting in a comfortable chair and that the room is quiet and at a pleasant temperature.

5. Ask easy, fact-gathering questions at the beginning.

For example, "Where and when were you born?" and "How long did you live there?" Save more emotionally charged questions like, "What was the most difficult challenge you've faced in your life?" for later in your interview.

6. Don't get locked into your list of questions.

It's more important to listen to your subject and follow up with questions that allow them to go deeper with their responses. Don't worry that you missed the next question on your list.

7. Ask questions that begin with How, When, Where and What.

These will elicit fuller answers than questions that lead to a one word Yes or No response. For example: If you ask, "Did you like your work?" The answer will likely be "Yes" or "No." But if you asked, "What did you like most (or least) about your work?" the possible reply might be, "Well, I really liked the fact that I could work from my home and be my own boss."

8. Three good follow-up questions:

"What do you mean by that?" "Can you tell me more? and "Can you give me some examples?"

9. Be engaged with your subject.

Look interested in their story…even if you're not!

8 How to Boost Your Interviewing Skills

In another section (24: Avoid These 3 Interviewing Pitfalls), I wrote about the need to go for depth when interviewing your subjects. What was missing from that article were examples of interview dialogue that could help you see the difference between poor interviews and good ones.

I've included two examples here. All the dialogue is made up. One example looks at the problem of jumping off the topic before exploring the subject's remarks fully. The second example highlights the problem of going into detail that does nothing to advance the story being told. It's the stories that are interesting. That's what we want to capture.

Example One: Jumping off the topic.

Poor

Interviewer: What was it like as a child growing up in a village?

Subject: Oh, we had some good times. Everyone knew everyone else.

Interviewer: That's wonderful. Tell me about the house you grew up in.

Better

Interviewer: What was it like as a child growing up in a village?

Subject: Oh, we had some good times. Everyone knew everyone else.

Interviewer: What were some of the good times you remember?

Subject: Well I remember in the fall we'd have the fall fair. People would come from all over. It had quite a reputation.

16

Interviewer: It sounds great. What were some of the things you enjoyed most about the fair? What is one of your most memorable stories about the fair?

…and so on

Example Two: Trivial details don't add up to depth.

Poor

Interviewer: What was special about your childhood home?

Subject: Oh it was located next to the prettiest little creek. In the summer we'd go swimming and in the winter skating.

Interviewer: What was the name of the creek?

Subject: I think it was called "Crystal Creek." Not sure though.

Interviewer: Do you think it was named after the clear water?

Subject: Maybe, although it wasn't too clear by the time it got to our place.

Interviewer: Where did the creek originate?

Subject: Not sure. I think it came out of Lake Clare.

Interviewer: How far was Lake Clare from you?

Subject: Maybe a mile or two.

Better

Interviewer: What was special about your childhood home?

Subject: Oh it was located next to the prettiest little creek. In the summer we'd go swimming and in the winter skating.

Interviewer: It does sound lovely. What's one of your most memorable stories about the creek?

Subject: Well I almost drowned!

Interviewer: Really! Tell me more.

Subject: It was in the early winter and the ice wasn't too thick. My parents had warned me to stay off the ice. But you know kids.

Interviewer: How old were you?

Subject: I think about six.

Interviewer: So what happened?

Subject: It was a bright sunny day and cold. I went down to the creek with my dog. The ice looked pretty thick so I decided to cross to the other side. I got about halfway and bang! I went through the ice! I tried hanging on the edge but I kept slipping away. I was really panicky and started shouting. What really saved me though was that my dog, Spotty, went rushing back to the house. He kept barking and my mom knew something was wrong. She followed him down to the creek. Without wasting any time she found a long branch on the ground and held it out to me to grab on to. She was a strong woman. She gave a great heave and I came sliding out and made my way back to the bank. She was pretty upset.

Interviewer: I bet! Then what happened?

…and so on

9 What I've Learned About Getting "Truthful" Interviews

Among personal historians the topic of honesty in interviews is a recurring topic. We want to ensure that our interviews illuminate the depth of a person's life and not simply skim across the surface. Questions arise about how far we should go to uncover the "truth" of a life lived.

I've done hundreds of interviews in my twenty-five years as a documentary filmmaker and personal historian. The interview subjects have included political leaders, prominent artists, historians, the dying, and the elderly.

This is what I've learned:

1. *People will tell me only what they are prepared to tell me.* No amount of clever or challenging questioning will change that fact. And I respect my client's wishes.

2. *The interview is not about my agenda and me.* My focus is always on my client and his or her needs.

3. *I must have the courage to ask reflective and sometimes difficult questions.* We owe it to our clients to raise questions that no one else may ask. "What have been the regrets in your life?" or "What are your fears around dying?" However, going back to my first point, I'm aware that asking the questions doesn't always elicit a full response.

4. *I am not a therapist.* My role is to help a person tell their story, not to make them better. I'm aware though that, through the process of interviewing, healing can occur for a client.

5. *Clients will sometimes reveal information to me that they have told no one.* Having revealed this information they may not want it preserved in print or video for the whole world to know and may ask that it be deleted.

6. *The degree to which people confide in me is directly proportional to the trust I'm able to establish.* This means that in my initial interviews I cover soft, easy topics like happy childhood memories or descriptions of a childhood home. Once the client and I have been together for a number of sessions, then I raise some of the more challenging questions.

7. *I'm not an investigative journalist.* Getting at the truth is critical for an investigative journalist. Compassion can be an impediment to their work. I'm a personal historian and my need for honesty is tempered by compassion for my client.

10 Do You Make These Interviewing Mistakes?

Interviewing a family member or a client for a personal history project involves more than just sitting down with a recorder and turning it on. Like anything done well, there is a real skill involved in drawing out the best stories. Here's a list of mistakes that lead to a poor interview. And believe me I know because over the years I've committed all of these at one time or another!

Not leaving room for silence.

This is especially important if you've asked a reflective question. Leave space for your subject to think. Don't leap in with another question.

Sitting too far away from your subject.

You want a degree of intimacy. This won't happen if you're sitting across the room. Make certain you're no more than five feet away from your subject.

Interrupting your subject.

Interrupting might work if you're a journalist trying to get at the heart of a hot story. But you're not. You're gathering a person's reminiscences about their life. Be gentle.

Talking about yourself.

The interview is not about you. Don't start relating how aspects of your life are just like your subject's.

Offering advice.

While you might be tempted to toss in some words of wisdom, don't. Your role is to unlock your subject's rich treasury of memories. You're not there as a therapist or counselor.

CHAPTER 2

Interviewing: Questions

11 How to Ask Questions That Will Unlock Life Stories

"A storyteller who provided us with...a profusion of details would rapidly grow maddening. Unfortunately, life itself often subscribes to this mode of storytelling, wearing us out with repetition, misleading emphases and inconsequential plot lines...The anticipatory and artistic imaginations omit and compress; they cut away the periods of boredom and direct our attention to critical moments, and thus, without either lying or embellishing, they lend to life a vividness and a coherence that it may lack in the distracting wooliness of the present." ~ Alain de Botton (The Art of Travel)

In my article How to Get the Stories in a Life Story Interview (6), I spoke about the need to draw on good storytelling techniques (e.g., surprising twists and turns, interesting characters, and a sense of progression) when interviewing a client for a life story.

In this article I want to focus on the kind of questions that will help unlock the stories.

What you want to think about as you're interviewing a client is *how do my questions help reveal the stories of this person's life.*

Avoid at all costs questions that lead to mind-numbing details that neither illustrate nor contribute to the story being told.

Now don't get me wrong. There's nothing inherently wrong with the minutiae of a life. But it must in some way enhance our appreciation of the overall story. For example, describing in some detail what an individual wore to school could nicely illustrate how poor this person was compared to fellow classmates.

On the other hand, details about where an interviewee bought his shoes, what kind of shoes they were, their color, how well they fit, and how much his friends admired them will cause our eyes to glaze over – unless there's a payoff.

To elicit stories use prompts such as *Describe, Illustrate, Paint, and Tell.*

To illustrate, I've grouped together six pairs of life story queries. The first in each pair is weaker than the second and on its own not likely to lead to much of a story. The second question is stronger and provides more opportunity for storytelling.

Weak   "Where did you live?"

Strong "Paint a picture for me of the place where you grew up."

Weak   "What did you do on summer holidays?"

Strong "What was one of your most memorable summer holidays?"

Weak   "What is your grandchild's name?"

Strong "Tell me a favorite story of you and your grandchild."

Weak   "What was a peak moment in your life?"

Strong "Describe a time when you felt on top of the world."

Weak   "What regrets do you have in your life?"

Strong "Describe an incident in your past that you still regret."

Weak   "What was the hardest part of being a parent?"

Strong "Tell me a story that illustrates the challenges of being a parent."

As personal historians we have an opportunity to turn the richness of a person's life into an engaging and treasured story. Remember the words of Ken Kesey: "To hell with facts! We need stories!"

12 Come to Your Senses and Unlock Childhood Memories

Nothing is more memorable than a smell. One scent can be unexpected, momentary and fleeting, yet conjure up a childhood summer beside a lake in the mountains ~ Diane Ackerman

How much do we remember from our childhood? This is one of the questions examined recently by Canadian research scientists.

I've just finished reading *Blanks for the Memories* which highlights aspects of the research originally published in the journal *Child Development*.

Neuroscientists believe that there are different kinds of memories, stored in many different neural circuits. "We can't go to a particular spot in the brain to see where our third birthday party is stored," says Dr. Hudson....

Scientists think the brain's prefrontal cortex processes experiences, using sensory input from the eyes, ears, nose and mouth, sorts them into categories, and tags the various memory fragments with specific associations (smells of home, friends from camp, bugs, a pet, for example).

Reading this made me realize how important the senses are to unlocking childhood memories. I must admit I could do a better job of incorporating sensory questions into my interviews. To get me pointed in the right direction, I've written a few sample "sensory" questions below.

I tested some out on my mother and she had great fun. It turns out that a taste she strongly associates with her childhood is jellybeans. Her mother would carefully count out five each for her and her two siblings. Today this may not sound like much but during the Great Depression, jellybeans were a real treat!

How much do you incorporate sense-related questions into your interviews? Do you have a favorite "sensory" question?

Sight

- What do you remember most about your mother's appearance?
- Paint a picture for me of where you lived—the weather, terrain.

Sound

- What sounds do you associate with your childhood? What memories do they evoke?
- What piece of music do you remember from your childhood?

Taste

- What was your favorite food when you were a child?
- What tastes do you associate with your childhood?

Touch

- What do you recall were things you loved to touch as a child?
- What do you remember liking to run your hands over or through?

Smell

- What are some of the pleasant smells you associate with your childhood? What memories do they bring back?

- What smells from your childhood weren't pleasant? What memories do they evoke?

13 Our Favorite Things Have Stories to Tell

Our treasured possessions are a window into the stories of our life.

Three years before she died, my frail, 91-year-old mother started to go through her modest collection of jewelry. She carefully tried to match each piece with a relative or friend she thought would appreciate having it after she died.

As I sat with her, she began telling me the stories behind each piece. There are the art deco black-and-white earrings she bought to go with a very fashionable dress my father got her shortly after they were married. A silver bracelet brought back by my dad from Pakistan during World War II is tarnished but her memories of my dad's war experiences remain vivid. Each piece unlocked a story in my mother's life.

And then there was a colleague at Victoria Hospice who told me of a unique funeral celebration he attended. A friend of the deceased gave a eulogy that was built entirely around photos of the shoes in the woman's life. Each pair of shoes had a story to tell.

In *The Globe and Mail* newspaper, I read an essay entitled "Family Ties." It tells the story of a son's remembrance of his father through the neckties that were passed down to him. Here's an excerpt:

> *The other day I was getting ready for work and went into my closet to get a tie...I reached for a striped tie and I remembered that it was one of my father's. He died last year and shortly afterward my mother, who was almost 80, made the decision to sell the big house we all grew up in. It took her a while, but she finally tackled the job of cleaning out my father's closets... My father had a lot of ties—dozens and dozens and dozens of them... And so, on this morning, I found myself knotting my father's tie, remembering how we stood in front of the mirror years ago, him teaching me how to get a half-Windsor just right. I smiled, knowing I might be the only person in the building that day with a tie on.*

Another interesting use of objects to tell a story appeared on the NPR website. Entitled "A Catalog—Literally—Of Broken Dreams," it reviews the book *Important Artifacts* by New York Times op-ed page art director Leanne Shapton. The NPR article points out:

> *Foregoing narrative entirely, Shapton tells the story of a couple's relationship in the form of a staggeringly precise ersatz auction catalog that annotates the common detritus of a love affair—notes, CD mixes, e-mails, photos, books—and places the objects up for sale... In choosing the conceit of an auction catalog, Shapton reminds us that the story of love*

can be told through the things we leave behind, but also by the condition in which we leave them.

All of this got me thinking. Wouldn't it be interesting to do a memoir or life story built around the special things someone possesses? Something to keep in mind.

14 Powerful Ways to Recall Forgotten Memories

I've been reading a remarkable book by Ojibway storyteller, Richard Wagamese. *One Native Life* is a memoir about roots and the power of recollection to heal. For anyone contemplating the writing of their own story or the story of another, I can't think of a better book to inspire you.

I was struck by a passage that made me realize how sound and light can be triggers for recalling forgotten memories. Wagamese writes,

> *The more I presented myself to the land in those early hours, the more it offered me back the realization of who I was created to be.*

> *I began to remember. The sound of squirrels in the topmost branches of a pine tree reminded me of a forgotten episode from my boyhood; the wobbly call of the loons took me back to an adventure on the land when I was a young man. And there was always the light. The shades and degrees of it evoked people and places I hadn't thought about in decades.*

Every one of those walks allowed me the grace of recollection,
and I began to write things down.

For me the lonely blast of a foghorn, the wild call of geese flying south
and the pounding surf on a rocky beach are just a few of the sounds that
can evoke strong memories of my childhood on the rugged West Coast
of Vancouver Island in British Columbia.

Wagamese's book has made me consider other ways our memories can
be triggered. Here are a few:

- *Smell.* One of the strongest memory triggers for me is the smell of
  baking bread. My mother always baked bread and today all I need
  is a whiff of freshly baked bread to take me back to some fond
  childhood memories. What odors evoke memories in you (or your
  client)?

- *Photographs.* Bring out the old photos and within minutes people
  will begin telling you the stories behind the images.

- *Music.* We all have a song or two that can trigger vivid memories.
  One of mine is Bob Dylan's "Blowin' In The Wind." I was a
  university student at the time this was popular and it became
  something of an anthem for me then. What's your song? What's
  your client's song?

- *A favorite object.* Everyone has a favorite object. And every object
  has a story to be told. Do you have a favorite object? Does your
  client?

- *A favorite childhood place.* This can be a place that was indoors or outdoors, rural or urban, fanciful or spiritual. What's the story behind your favorite place? What's your client's favorite place?

When writing, or when interviewing a client, keep in mind these powerful ways to tap into the rich treasury of memories that lie just below the surface of our awareness.

15 Are You Asking the Courageous Questions?

"The key point [of my interviews] was empathy because everybody in their lives is really waiting for people to ask them questions, so that they can be truthful about who they are and how they became what they are." ~ Marc Pachter, Cultural Historian

Marc Pachter founded Living Self-Portraits at the Smithsonian and was its master interviewer. In his TED talk below he shares the challenges of getting a good interview.

"...if all you're going to get from the interviewee is their public self, there's no point in it. It's pre-programmed. It's infomercial, and we all have infomercials about our lives. We know the great lines, we know the great moments, we know what we're not going to share ..."

Marc recounts several interviews and how he cut below the surface conversation to have his subjects reveal the truth of their lives.

31

Marc's talk reminds me of the advice I give to those I train for life story interviewing. I tell my students they need to ask the "courageous questions." These are the questions that people have been waiting to be asked all of their lives. It requires courage on both sides. The interviewer must be confident enough to raise the questions. The interviewee must be unafraid to answer them.

Our work as personal historians, unlike Marc Pachter's, seldom involves the famous. But the need to go beyond the pre-programmed responses is the same. How do we do that in a way that's both incisive and empathetic? Here are some clues.

Trust your intuition.

Intuition is that ability of knowing without any rational explanation—a kind of sixth sense. I've talked about this to some degree in another article (20: How to Listen with Your Eyes).

When we're engaged in an interview, it's not just the words we're listening to but also the subtext. It's the eyes that give us clues to what's behind the words. Our subject may express happiness and contentment but the eyes are sad. We may hear kindness and openness but the eyes are angry and narrowed. If we're doing our job well, we need to check out this dissonance with our interviewee. By listening with our eyes we unearth a richer, more authentic story.

Trusting your intuition and blurting out what we sense doesn't mean that it's always right. And that's okay. People will set you straight if you've missed the mark.

As a rule, I generally preface my hunches with something like, "I have this feeling and I might be totally off base but I'd like to check it out..." [followed by the courageous question.]

With time and practice we can begin to trust our intuition and put it at the service of our clients.

Acknowledge the elephant.

An elephant in the room can crush the intimacy from an interview. To help people express themselves and as Pachter says "to feel what they ... [want] to say and to be an agent of their self-revelation" we need to be fearless in acknowledging the elephant.

The caveat is that we must always be clear on our intent. We are the means through which people can speak unburdened. Our intent is not to embarrass, intimidate, or expose the interviewee.

For example, in my work I've found that most of those at the end of life welcome an opportunity to talk about their fears and hopes. But I also know that it's not uncommon for friends and family of terminally-ill patients to avoid the subject of death altogether. While it's perfectly understandable, such silence can leave the dying feeling even more isolated.

Be curious.

Curiosity is one of the key tools in an interviewer's toolkit. It's both playful and disarming. The question begins with "I wonder or I'm curious..." and invites an exploration between you and the interviewee.

Questions that are asked out of curiosity usually lead to responses that are authentic and deep.

For example, after listening to your interviewee go on and on about their terrible childhood you might ask, "You've painted such a bleak picture of your childhood, I was wondering what were some of the good things that you can recall?"

Such a question stops the interviewee from the pre-programmed infomercial described by Marc Pachter and gives the person an opportunity to dig deeper and uncover some bright spots.

Conclusion

As personal historians we owe it to our clients to ask the courageous questions. One's life story is more than a sterile recitation of dates, names, places, and events. Ultimately it's about the complexity and richness of a soul's journey. Courageous questions unlock this richness and give heart and substance to a personal history.

16 The 50 Best Life Story Questions

Of all the posts on my blog, this list was by far the most popular.

1. If you could do one thing over in your life, what would it be?
2. What makes you happy?
3. Looking back on your life, what do you regret?
4. What do you believe to be true?

5. What is the secret to a happy life?

6. What do you believe happens to us after we die?

7. Who's had the greatest influence on your life and why?

8. What are the qualities that you admire in your friends?

9. What is the hardest thing you've ever had to do?

10. How would you describe yourself?

11. If you could meet anyone in the world, who would it be and why?

12. What's important in your life?

13. If you had a million dollars, what would you do with it?

14. What's a secret ambition of yours?

15. Who in your life would you like to thank and for what?

16. What principles have guided your life?

17. Where do you find serenity?

18. What makes you sad?

19. What's the most important lesson you've learned in your life?

20. How would you like to be remembered?

21. If you had only one day to live, how would you live it?

22. How would you describe your spiritual beliefs?

23. Who is the most important person in your life today and why?

24. What was the worst job you ever had and why was it so bad?

25. What's your idea of a good time?

26. What's wrong with the world?

27. What's one big question you'd like answered?

28. What is it that you absolutely couldn't live without?

29. How would you describe yourself as a child?

30. What's the greatest gift you could give to someone you love?

31. What does love mean to you?

32. What was the best job you ever had and why was it the best?

33. If you had to evacuate your home immediately and could take only one thing, what would it be and why?

34. What do you still want to accomplish?

35. What's right with the world?

36. What's one thing you'd like to change about yourself?

37. How would you describe your perfect day?

38. What event in your life would you like to live over and why?

39. What are you avoiding?

40. What are your best qualities?

41. What's the most romantic thing you've done for someone?

42. Who are your heroes and why?

43. What are your failings?

44. What's the kindest thing you've done for someone?

45. What is more important to you, challenge or comfort, and why?

46. How is your home like you?

47. If your life were a motion picture, what would the title be?

48. Who in your life would you like to forgive and for what?

49. What are the advantages of getting older?

50. What would you place in a time capsule that would tell a relative 100 years from now who you were?

17 The 50 Best Questions to Ask Your Mother

How well do you really know your mother? Chances are, not as well as you think.

Why not consider putting together a little recording or booklet about your mother? The following questions are a good place to start.

[Note: These questions assume a traditional family with Mom, Dad, and children. I'm aware that the wording of several questions might feel exclusionary for same sex partners with children. That's not my intent. The questions can be easily adapted to fit any family.]

1. Describe who you were as a little girl.
2. What's a favorite story from your childhood?
3. What did you learn from your parents?
4. How are you like and different from your mother?
5. How are you like and different from your father?
6. Other than your parents, who was the most important person in your life when you were a child? And why?
7. What's a favorite memory from your elementary school days?
8. As a young girl, what did you dream of being one day?
9. How did your childhood shape the woman you are today?
10. Tell me a story that involves you and your first boyfriend.
11. As an adolescent, what kind of mischief did you get into?
12. Tell me about your first job.
13. What did you work at the longest and what did you like about it?

14. What didn't you like about that job?

15. Tell me how you and Dad met?

16. What attracted you to him?

17. What did you hope for in your married life?

18. How did your married life meet your expectations?

19. How are you and Dad alike and different?

20. Tell me a story about a special time in your marriage.

21. What have you learned about marriage that you'd like to pass on to others?

22. How did having children change your life?

23. What's the best and worst thing about being a mother?

24. What words of wisdom do you have on parenting?

25. What was an important road not taken?

26. What have you been the proudest of in your life?

27. Tell me a story that shows how you overcame an obstacle in your life.

28. What would you say are your weaknesses?

29. What's a dream not yet fulfilled?

30. What do you rely on to get you through the tough times?

31. Describe a moment in your life that was filled with wonder.

32. Who's been the most important person in your adult life? And why?

33. How would you describe your spiritual beliefs?

34. What's your view of an afterlife?

35. What has always come easy to you?

36. What are your three wishes for me?

37. What do you admire about me?

38. If you had one piece of advice for me, what would it be?

39. What qualities do you admire in your friends?

40. If you could change one thing in the world, what would it be? And why?

41. What makes you laugh?

42. What makes you sad?

43. Whom do you admire most in the world? And why?

44. What was the happiest time in your life?

45. What's unique about you?

46. If you could change one thing in your life, what would that be?

47. What's the most amazing thing you've experienced in your life?

48. Tell me something that people don't know about you.

49. If you had only one day to live, how would you live it?

50. How would you like to be remembered?

If you found these questions helpful, you might also want to look at The 50 Best Life Story Questions (16).

CHAPTER 3:

Interviewing: Listening

18 How to Be An Engaged Listener

I've written elsewhere about useful techniques for interviewing: How to Listen With Your Third Ear (19) and 9 Secrets of a Good Interview (7). "The interview" is a key component of a life story project. Being a good interviewer means being an engaged listener.

Here are six tips that'll help you become more engaged with the person you're interviewing.

1. Establish eye contact.

Don't fix your subject with a "steely" stare but do check to make certain you're not gazing off into the distance.

2. Use appropriate facial expressions.

If the story you're hearing is funny, smile or laugh. If it's serious or sad, look compassionate. Nod your head to signal you understand or agree with what's being said.

3. Use verbal cues.

In order to indicate that you're actually listening use expressions such as:

- "I see."
- "Uh, huh."
- "Interesting."
- "Mmm."
- "Wow."

4. Ask for clarification.

Don't be afraid to interrupt politely and ask your subject to explain something that's not clear to you. If it's not clear to you, chances are it's not going to be clear to others.

5. Provide a brief recap or summary.

This should be used judiciously—after a pause or before you move on to another topic. Summarizing demonstrates that you're actively listening. It will sometimes prompt your subject to add more detail or explain more clearly.

6. Acknowledge.

If your subject has just finished telling you a touching or revealing story, don't abruptly move on to your next question. Make sure you pause and add a sentence or two that acknowledges your subject's feelings. For example, if you've been told about a lifelong regret over not completing university studies, you might say something like, "I can see that you've struggled with this for a long time. It must be very hard."

19 How to Listen With Your Third Ear

Over the years I've trained novices in the art of the interview. I've noticed that inexperienced interviewers are frequently missing what I'd call their Third Ear. I'm not talking about steroid-induced mutant ears. This is about listening at a deeper level than we are accustomed to doing.

At a basic level we hear the words being spoken to us. With our Third Ear we pick up what isn't being said. We notice the missing content and we intuitively sense that there is more going on than appears on the surface. The most effective interviewers are those who've mastered the use of their Third Ear.

Let's look at a sample of fictional interview dialogue to illustrate my point. Sample A shows an interviewer without the Third Ear.

Sample A

Interviewer: When was a time you felt most alive?

Subject: Times when I was most engaged in the moment.

Interviewer: I see. Tell me more.

Subject: Well, when the world was my oyster.

Interviewer: Right. Your oyster. My next question is about regrets.

Now let's look at the same interview but with an interviewer using the Third Ear.

Sample B

> Interviewer: When was a time you felt most alive?
>
> Subject: Times when I was most engaged in the moment.
>
> Interviewer: When would have been a time when you felt engaged in the moment?
>
> Subject: Well, when the world was my oyster.
>
> Interviewer: Give me an example of when the world was your oyster.
>
> Subject: Well the time I received a prominent award for my book. I was the toast of the town. Everyone wanted to interview me. It was great!
>
> Interviewer: That does sound fantastic. I may be wrong but I sense that it wasn't all wonderful.
>
> Subject: Yeah, you're right. It eventually led to some real strains on my marriage.

I hope the distinction between the two samples is clear. In Sample A, the interviewer doesn't go for detail and misses out on an important aspect of the story. On the other hand, in Sample B the interviewer digs deeper for concrete examples and relies on her intuition to uncover a richer story.

Developing your Third Ear takes time and practice. It requires that you be fully present and focused on what your interview subject is saying. And it means that you have to cut through vague, general statements and get to specific details. This, combined with trusting your intuition, will begin to pay off in better interviews.

20 How to Listen with Your Eyes

An eye can threaten like a loaded and leveled gun, or it can insult like hissing or kicking; or, in its altered mood, by beams of kindness, it can make the heart dance for joy. ... One of the most wonderful things in nature is a glance of the eye; it transcends speech; it is the bodily symbol of identity. ~ Ralph Waldo Emerson

I had the pleasure of moderating a documentary film presentation and panel discussion at the 16th annual Association of Personal Historians conference.

The session featured the screening of *Ted Grant: The Art of Observation* followed by a Q&A with the audience, the film's subject Ted Grant, and writer, co-producer, and co-director Heather MacAndrew.

Ted Grant is the dean of Canadian photojournalism; his career spans over five decades. In the documentary I was struck by an observation Ted made: "We hear with our ears but we listen with our eyes."

Ted's comment got me thinking. As personal historians, the root of our work is the interview. When we're interviewing then, how do we listen, as Ted says, with our eyes?

When we're engaged in an interview, it's not just the words we're listening to but also the subtext. It's the eyes that give us clues to what's behind the words. Our subject may express happiness and contentment but the eyes are sad. We may hear kindness and openness but the eyes are angry and narrowed. If we're doing our job well, we need to check out this dissonance with our interviewee.

By listening with our eyes we unearth a richer more authentic story.

If our interviewees are speaking volumes with their eyes, what are we conveying to them through our eyes? I'm sure we've all had the experience of talking to someone who appears to be listening. They're facing us, their head is nodding appropriately, they're making sounds of acknowledgment, and yet something tells us they aren't there with us. What's going on? A clue is in the eyes. They're unfocused and distant. Now ask yourself this. "When interviewing someone who isn't particularly interesting, what are my eyes conveying?" If I'm honest with myself, more than likely my eyes are saying, "Dan's not here."

There are other examples. If we're feeling nervous about a particular interview or anxious about a family matter, our eyes will reflect our internal state. Pretending that all is well will send mixed signals. Our failure to get a good interview may in part be a result of the conflicting messages we're conveying to our interview subjects.

Our ability to draw out the best from our clients depends so much on our ability to listen deeply. Thank you Ted Grant for reminding us that as interviewers we do indeed hear with our ears but listen with our eyes.

21 How to Use "Acknowledgment" to Build a Better Interview

I find the use of "acknowledgment" in a personal history interview one way to build rapport with my interviewee. It's a particularly effective technique after you've been told a touching story.

Imagine you've just listened to a charming recounting of a woman's first dance date. She ends by saying, "Oh, it was so much fun!" You could remark, "Yes, it sounds delightful." But even better would be to say something like:

> *I can sense that. When you described picking out the blue dress you wore, your initial nervousness about how you looked, your handsome date, and the great music, I could see from the glow on your face that this was a very special event. It's wonderful that you still have such a vivid recollection of it.*

By briefly summarizing what you heard and letting your subject know that you appreciate and understand her, you're using "acknowledgment" and fostering trust.

But "acknowledgment" can do so much more. This pause to acknowledge your interviewee's anecdote is also the perfect point to inject a more probing question. For example, continuing with the illustration above, you could say:

> *...It's wonderful that you still have such a vivid recollection of it. So what do you recall about your date that didn't work out so well?*

Your interviewee might have nothing to add. On the other hand your question might unlock a really interesting story.

If you feel there's a need to move your interviewee along to another topic, acknowledgment can provide a natural break. For example:

> *...It's wonderful that you still have such a vivid recollection of it. I'd like to turn our attention now to your family life when you were a teenager. I know you were an only child. What did you miss about not having siblings?*

Acknowledging what you have just heard before changing course in the interview makes your interviewee feel listened to and recognized. And as a result the person is more willing to allow you to steer the interview in another direction.

Like any technique, you don't want to overuse "acknowledgment." But I find it's a valuable tool to have in my interview kit bag.

22 Want To Do A Better Job of Listening?

So when you are listening to somebody, completely, attentively, then you are listening not only to the words, but also to the feeling of what is being conveyed, to the whole of it, not part of it. ~ Jiddu Krishnamurti (1895 – 1986), spiritual philosopher

At the heart of a good interview is your ability to be an active listener – to listen, as Krishnamurti notes, to the whole of what someone says, not just the words. Here are seven things you can do that will help you do a better job of listening.

1. Acknowledging

- *Non-verbal:* an open relaxed body position, facing the person squarely, eye contact, nodding and appropriate emotional response, e.g., smiling, sad, or curious. Use of silence to give your subject time to think and reflect.

- Verbal: "I see." "Uh, huh." "Okay." "Yeah." "Oh, really."

2. Questioning

- Use open questions, How? What? Where? When? rather than closed questions that lead to yes or no responses. Example: Closed – "Did that affect you?" Open – "How did that affect you?"

- Stay away from "Why" questions that can make a person feel defensive.

- Avoid an interrogating style and aim for a conversational tone that is calm and gentle.

- Ask one question at a time and keep questions short and simple.

3. Suspending judgment

- Refrain from verbal expressions of disapproval. Don't use words such as "should," "ought," or "must."

- Avoid non-verbal disapproval. Don't grimace or shake your head or cast your eyes heavenward.

- Don't give opinions unless asked.

4. Concentrating

- Leave your concerns outside the door and be fully present.

- Focus on your subject and be alert to when your mind wanders. Gently bring it back to the "here and now."

5. Supporting

- Express warmth and caring in a personal and appropriate way.

- Don't interrupt.

6. Clarifying

When you're not clear about what your subject said, ask for clarification or paraphrase what they've said to be certain you've understood the person correctly.

7. Summarizing

Pulling together feelings, experiences, ideas and facts without adding any new ideas helps provide a sense of movement to the interview. It also demonstrates to your subject your ability to listen attentively to what has been said and as a result builds trust.

CHAPTER 4:

Interviewing: Challenges

23 4 Ways to Get Control of a Runaway Interview

A weakness common to novice interviewers is their inability to take charge of an interview. Interviews frequently look like a runaway train with the interviewer gamely hanging on to the proverbial little red caboose.

Taking charge doesn't mean forcing or dictating the direction of the interview. It's more like riding a horse. Anyone familiar with riding knows that it requires confidence and a gentle hold on the reins. The same approach applies to interviewing.

Here are four ways to keep control of your interview:

1. From the outset, be clear what you want from the interview.

If you're clear before you start on the topic you want to explore and its parameters, then it is easier to stay on track.

For example, if you know you want to capture a client's childhood stories about summer holidays, then start your interview by saying something like, "Tom, today I'd like you to think back to your childhood and your summer holidays. What's a particularly strong memory of the games you played?"

2. Use short, focused questions.

The more precise your questions the more specific the answers from your interviewees. For example, a good question would be "What was your Mother's special gift or talent?" A poor question would be "Tell me about your family."

Questions that aren't specific make interviewees anxious because they don't know what you're searching for. If you continue to follow-up with vague, unfocused questions, their trust will erode and so will the interview.

3. Gently interrupt.

It's difficult, I know. It seems somehow impolite. But you'd be surprised how many people really don't mind being interrupted in an interview. In fact they appreciate that you're paying attention and bringing them back on topic.

Wait for your interviewee to pause before interrupting politely. For example, "Margaret, this is a fascinating story about your aunt. Later we'll be taking more time to talk about your extended family. But I'd like to come back to the earlier question I asked about your mother."

It's important to acknowledge the interviewees' remarks, assure them that the topic will be covered, and then gently nudge them back on track.

4. Go where there's passion.

Sometimes it's best to throw your plans out the window. An apparently innocent question on your part might trigger a strong emotional response in your interviewees that has no apparent connection to your question. If this happens, take the time to explore the story behind the emotion.

Clearly your interviewees want to talk about this now. If you put them off by forcing them back on topic, you can lose a really important story.

Conclusion

If you're just starting out as a professional personal historian, I hope these suggestions will be helpful. Use them as guidelines—not as hard and fast rules. Interviewing is more an art than a science. With experience comes an intuitive sense of how to guide an interview and get the best possible story.

24 Avoid These 3 Interviewing Pitfalls

A good interview is at the heart of any personal history. I train and mentor hospice volunteers in Victoria on the art of life story interviewing. It's part of a program being offered by Victoria Hospice. I've found several interviewing pitfalls that I suspect are universal to those new to the craft. Here's a look at three:

1. Losing control of the interview.

Losing control is particularly easy with very talkative subjects. Novices let their subjects ramble without knowing how to interrupt and put the interview back on track.

Solution: Before the interview even starts, you need to be clear in your own mind what you want to get from the interview. When you begin, say something like: "Mary, today we're going to be covering your early school days. I'd like to start by asking you...."

You must be fearless. Step in when your subject strays off topic. Some meandering can be useful. But if it becomes a regular occurrence and it consists of "fluff," you've got to interrupt. Some of you may be concerned about seeming insensitive. However, you can interrupt with a smile on your face. You might say something like, "I'm sorry to interrupt, Mary, but I feel we've kind of strayed off topic. Your stories about your next door neighbor are interesting but I'd like to bring you back to your early childhood, especially your remembrance of school days."

From my experience, people are okay with this. You owe it to your client not to waste their time and money with a lot of extraneous material.

2. Lost in minutiae.

Your subject may get caught up in details that have nothing to do with illuminating or advancing the story. For example, it can be useful to know the layout and look of a childhood home. This can help evoke memories, especially if the details are around a favorite room. What's of less interest is what color rooms were painted or whether some had wallpaper and some had carpets. (Unless of course there's some interesting story to do with the color or wallpaper or carpets.)

Solution: Avoid going down the rabbit hole of trivia. Stop yourself from asking questions that elicit more useless bits of information. And how will you know if it's useless? Ask yourself, "Does this information explain or describe some activity or mechanism that would be of interest to someone in the future? Is this detail helping to paint a fuller picture of my subject? Can I use this information to draw out a story from my subject?" If your answer to these questions is NO, then it's time to pull the plug and refocus the interview.

3. Failing to get below the surface.

I find most subjects have stock responses to stock questions. It's not that the interviewee is being facile. It's more that no one has ever asked the person a really thought-provoking question. If we skip along the surface, we may learn for example that "Mary" had a loving family and happy childhood, went to school, and then got married. And really that's about it, except for a lot of filler. This doesn't make for a rich and satisfying life story.

Solution: I teach my students to be always listening for what's not being said. So for example, if Mary waxes on about how her childhood was charming, at some point you want to say, "Mary, it sounds like you had a wonderful childhood. What were some of the hard times?" Or let's say Mary has been painting a gloomy picture of her childhood. Then you'll want to say, "Mary, it sounds like you had a tough childhood. What were some of the good things that happened?" or "How did this difficult childhood make you the person you are today?"

Powerful questions are the ones that stop people in their tracks and make them think. You'll know when you've asked such a question. Your interviewee will stop, take a deep breath, look at you in silence, and then give her answer. And don't be surprised if she says, "That's a great question! I never thought of that before."

25 How to Interview a "Challenging" Subject

I've always found it relatively easy to interview someone who is outgoing and an extrovert. The challenge is interviewing someone who is more withdrawn and tends to respond with one word or one sentence answers. It's like pulling teeth to get their story. If it's an older person who is also hard of hearing and has poor vision, it can make the interview that much more difficult.

So how do you interview a challenging subject? Here's what I've learned over the years.

- *Select a favorite spot.* Make certain that your interview takes place in a room where your subject is comfortable. If she has a favorite chair or spot in the house, use that location for the interview.

- *Engage in some idle "chit-chat."* Before sitting down to the interview, talk about the weather, sports, their art work—anything that allows your subject to feel more relaxed with you.

- *Remain calm.* If your subject senses you're anxious about not getting much from the interview, she's likely to become even less responsive.

- *Leave some space.* After your subject has responded to your question with a brief word or two, don't leap in with another probing question in an attempt to get more out of him. Count to ten. Sometimes just leaving space makes people want to fill it in. If you're lucky, your subject will start to add some more detail.

- *Create a picture for your subject.* Don't ask, "What was your childhood home like?" Start by saying something like, "I want you to paint a picture of your childhood home for me. So we're standing outside the front of your home and walking up to the front door. We open it and go inside. Tell me, what do we see as we go inside?" After some description of the entrance go on with, "That's wonderful. Now let's explore further. As we're going down the hall what do we see?"

- *Be specific.* Avoid very general questions like, "What was your childhood like?" Chances are the response will be, "Oh, it was

56

okay." You want to get details. Ask something like, "I want you to think back to those memories of childhood when you were with your father. It might have been at play or at the supper table. Think back and select a moment that is vivid for you. [pause] Okay? Now describe for me where you were and what was happening."

- *Use open-ended questions.* Open questions begin with who, what, where and when. For example, let's say your subject replies, "It was a good marriage" to your question of, "What was your married life like?" You can go further by asking, "How was it good?" This requires your subject to provide some specifics.

- *For those who are hard of hearing, speak clearly and slowly.* You need to make sure your questions are actually being heard. It seems obvious to say "speak loudly" but I find interviewers tend to go quiet on questions that are of an intimate or sensitive nature. You don't need to shout but you do need to project your voice— like a stage actor.

26 Can Life Stories Benefit Those With Alzheimer's?

Some years ago, when I was a filmmaker, I did a documentary on family caregivers. The show dealt with five caregivers, two of whom were struggling to look after a parent suffering from Alzheimer's disease. I had a close-up look at the challenges the disease inflicts on patient and caregiver alike. When I became a personal historian, I felt there was therapeutic value in recording the life stories of those with Alzheimer's.

Soon after starting my personal history work, I had the opportunity to do a series of video interviews for a charming and accomplished woman who was at an early stage of Alzheimer's. Both she and her family realized that if I didn't get the stories recorded they would soon be lost forever. She thoroughly enjoyed my visits and seemed stimulated by the recall of familiar stories from her past. Today that same woman has deteriorated considerably but her family finds some comfort in knowing that her life lives on in these recordings we made.

An article on MayoClinic.com ("Alzheimer's: Mementos help preserve memories") seems to bear out my anecdotal observations about the value of life stories and Alzheimer's:

"Caregivers become the memory for their loved one with Alzheimer's disease," says Glenn Smith, Ph.D., a neuropsychologist at Mayo Clinic, Rochester, Minn. "By gathering memories, you can bring important events and experiences from your loved one's past into the present. You're the link to his or her life history....By creating a life story, you affirm for your loved one all the positive things he or she has done in life and can still do. Even after your relative's memories start to fade, creating a life story shows that you value and respect his or her legacy. It also reminds you who your loved one was before Alzheimer's disease."

Tom Kitwood (in his groundbreaking 1997 book *Dementia Reconsidered*) believes that a life history book for a person with dementia, complete with photographs, should become best practice. He says, "In dementia a sense of identity based on having a life story to tell may eventually fade. When it does, biographical knowledge about a person becomes essential if that identity is still to be held in place."

If you know a family member at an early stage of Alzheimer's disease, you might give serious consideration to recording their life story. If you're a professional personal historian unsure if you should work with clients who have dementia, give it serious consideration. You could be providing a wonderful gift.

Web related resources:

- Alzheimer's Association (USA) (http://www.alz.org/)
- Alzheimer Society (Canada) (http://www.alzheimer.ca/en)

- The Fisher Center For Alzheimer's Research Foundation (http://www.alzinfo.org/)

27 How to Interview Someone with Dementia

Over the years I've interviewed individuals with dementia brought about by Alzheimer's or small cerebral strokes. What I've learned I felt might be of value to those of you facing a similar challenge of interviewing someone with dementia.

Keep in mind that in advanced stages of Alzheimer's it is virtually impossible to conduct an effective interview.

Here then are my suggestions:

- Be flexible with your interview schedule. Your interviewees might have days when they're simply not up to being interviewed.
- Be patient and avoid completing sentences for the person.
- Speak clearly and slowly.
- Ask one uncomplicated question at a time. You may have to repeat the question.
- Keep the interview time short. Elderly, sick people usually exhaust easily.
- Focus on one topic. Focusing allows you to get at missing details from different perspectives.
- Don't niggle over a name or date. Reassure the interviewee that, "It's okay. We'll worry about that later." Be aware that names,

places, and dates that the interviewee provides might be inaccurate. If you can verify these with someone in the family, that would be helpful.

- Have a transcript prepared of your interview session and at your next meeting have the interviewee read it over, if they can still read. Reading it might prompt some memory recall.

- Refresh the interviewee's memory of your last interview. Something like, "Yesterday you told me about your dad. You said he was a stern man. What more can you say about your father?"

- One of the last things to go with many dementia victims is their musical memory. Perhaps some musical selection, a favorite tune, might spark some memories. It's worth a try.

- It could be useful to have a family member present to help prompt some memories.

CHAPTER 5:

Interviewing: Self-Test

28 How Good Are Your Interviewing Skills?

Try this short self-assessment. You'll get a sense of your strengths and weaknesses as a personal history interviewer. My suggestion would be to work from a printed copy.

This is adapted from a larger self-assessment that I developed for use by our Life Stories volunteers at Victoria Hospice.

1. I listen to my previous recorded interview with the storyteller and make notes on additional questions I want to ask.

    always almost always sometimes never

 2. I prepare a list of questions I want to cover before my next interview session.

    always almost always sometimes never

3. I can leave my troubles at the door and concentrate on the storyteller.

always   almost always   sometimes   never

4. I ensure that the storyteller is as comfortable as possible for the interview.

always   almost always   sometimes   never

5. I ensure that all audio distractions such as telephones, radios, TVs, and music players are turned off.

always   almost always   sometimes   never

6. I try my best to make sure that there are no other people in the room when I'm interviewing the storyteller.

always   almost always   sometimes   never

7. As much as possible, I use open-ended questions which start with: Who, What, When, Where, How, and sometimes Why.

always   almost always   sometimes   never

8. I provide appropriate supportive non-verbal listening such as nodding, smiling, frowning, leaning forward, and maintaining "non-intense" eye contact.

always   almost always   sometimes   never

9. I use supportive verbal acknowledgment sparingly. This includes such expressions as: I see. Yes. Mmm. Right. Of course. Really. Tell me more. That must have been very difficult.

always   almost always   sometimes   never

10. I keep an open mind and don't mentally judge the storyteller's remarks.

always   almost always   sometimes   never

11. I ask only one question at a time.

always   almost always   sometimes   never

12. If I don't understand what has been said, I ask the storyteller for clarification.

always   almost always   sometimes   never

13. When appropriate during the interview, I recap what the storyteller has told me.

always   almost always   sometimes   never

14. If possible, I face the storyteller and sit no more than five feet away.

always   almost always   sometimes   never

15. I speak in a clear voice and loud enough to be heard by the storyteller and picked up by the recorder mic.

always   almost always   sometimes   never

16. If I sense resistance to a question, I don't force the storyteller to answer.

always   almost always   sometimes   never

17. I easily admit to being at a loss for the next question and suggest time out.

always   almost always   sometimes   never

18. When I become aware that a response by the storyteller could cause others discomfort, I pause the recorder. I remind the storyteller that others will hear their remarks. I then ask if the storyteller wishes me to continue recording or switch to a different topic.

always almost always sometimes never

19. I'm comfortable with sad, tearful moments.

always almost always sometimes never

20. For the most part, I don't ask questions from a list, preferring to use it as back up.

always almost always sometimes never

21. I'm genuinely curious and encourage the storyteller to provide more detail and texture to stories. I temper this with a need to balance time constraints and to honor the storyteller's wishes regarding disclosure.

always almost always sometimes never

22. If I'm recording potentially revelatory stories, I make certain that as soon as possible I acknowledge on the recording that the storyteller has given me permission to record this material.

always almost always sometimes never

23. I know when I'm encountering emotionally charged stories that are beyond my ability and expertise to handle.

always almost always sometimes never

24. I'm comfortable suggesting to the storyteller that the person might wish to speak to a counselor.

always   almost always   sometimes   never

25. I gently bring the storyteller back to the topic at hand if the person has strayed into material that is of little or no interest.

always   almost always   sometimes   never

26. If the storyteller begins to use the interview as an opportunity to malign someone, I stop the recording. I explain that this is not appropriate and that I will not proceed if the storyteller insists on expressing such comments.

always   almost always   sometimes   never

27. I am more concerned about getting the stories behind a life than the facts of the story.

always   almost always   sometimes   never

28. At the end of the interview session I thank the storyteller for taking the time to share memories.

always   almost always   sometimes   never

CHAPTER 6:

Audio-Video

29 The Secret to Recording Audio Like the Pros

How would you like your voice to be remembered? If it were recorded for posterity, you'd want the audio to be crystal clear, natural, and devoid of background distractions.

As personal historians we owe it to our clients to record the best quality audio interviews possible. I know some of you may be saying, "But I produce books and so the audio isn't critical. I only use the audio for transcription purposes."

I beg to differ. For families, hearing the voice of a loved one years after their death is a special gift. So even if you just produce books, it's still essential to provide your clients with an archival set of well-recorded interviews. Sound counts. Don't mess it up!

I learned about producing high quality audio recordings from the sound technician I used on my early documentaries. At first he drove me nuts with his perfectionism. But I learned valuable lessons from him that I still apply to my personal history interviews today.

Here's how to record like a pro:

Use a top-notch digital audio recorder.

Good sound starts with good equipment and there are many choices out there. Among personal historians there are those who favor the Marantz recorders—PMD 661, PMD 620, or PMD 660. Some like the Fostex FR2-LE. The Zoom H4 and H2 are popular with others. All are good choices with the nod going to those that have XLR microphone inputs. These inputs allow for the use of top-quality professional mics.

The bottom line is to use the best recorder your budget can afford.

Use a high quality microphone.

Don't rely on the built-in microphones on your audio recorders or cameras. Trust me, they produce poor sound. Buy the best condenser lavaliere (lapel) omnidirectional microphone you can afford. Expect to pay from $100 to $400. Quality costs but you won't regret it.

Why an omnidirectional condenser mic? The sound quality for interview purposes is better than with a directional microphone.

For more information on microphones check out these articles:

- Which Lavaliere Should I Use? (http://tinyurl.com/45fo7d)
- Guide to Lavaliere Microphones (http://tinyurl.com/nnm9goh)

Record in a quiet environment.

Stay indoors. It's nearly impossible to control outdoor sounds what with planes, car horns, kids shouting, loud birds, and wind. Inside a home, find the quietest room. It's usually the living room or bedroom because of the carpeted floors and draped windows. Make sure to pull the drapes closed and shut the door. The more sound-absorbing surfaces that surround you, the better the sound.

Take a moment to listen for any unwanted background sounds—ticking clocks, air conditioner or furnace fans, refrigerator, fluorescent light buzz, radio or TV, computer hum. Ask your interviewee if you might turn these "noise generators" off. And don't forget to disconnect the telephone! A word of caution. Before leaving, make sure you've turned everything back on.

A great tip from fellow APH member Dave Morrison: If you turn off a noisy refrigerator, put your car keys inside so that you do NOT leave without turning the box back on.

Always use headphones.

You can't monitor the audio without wearing a good set of headphones. My advice is to use circumaural headphones—ones that go fully around the ear. This type of headphone is comfortable to wear and produces quality sound. Sony, Audio-Technica, and Sennheiser are good makes. Expect to pay between $100 and $200 for an entry-level headphone.

Listen for unwanted background sounds such as those mentioned above. In addition, be attentive for your interviewee popping "P's" or producing sibilant "S's." Moving the lapel mic so that it's not in a direct line with the subject's mouth can sometimes help.

Run a short test of your equipment.

Before leaving for your interview check your recorder, mic, and headphones to ensure everything is working properly. Once you're at your interviewee's home, take a moment to test the audio. Ask your subject an easy question such as, "Tell me about a favorite meal of yours" or "Describe the room we're sitting in." Stop and replay the recording, listening carefully to the quality of the sound. If it's clear and free of unwanted noise, you're good to go.

Conclusion

Poor audio is the mark of an amateur. You don't have to spend a fortune to get a good recorder, microphone, and headphone. And you can quickly learn to monitor your recording environment to get the best sound possible. By following these tips you'll record audio like a pro and leave your clients with a treasured audio legacy.

30 Do You Make These 5 Common Audio Mistakes?

Imagine yourself in this situation. You've just completed videotaping an hour-long interview. It was nicely lit and framed. And the interview itself was fantastic! Excitedly you rush back to your editing suite, put up your interview to screen, and then the shock. The picture looks great but the audio is terrible. There's nothing you can do to fix it. The interview is ruined!

I know that getting flawless sound all the time is nearly impossible. But you can improve the odds if you avoid making these 5 common audio mistakes.

1. Using the wrong microphone.

All microphones are not created equal. The worst choice is using the microphone that comes with your video or audio recorder. These are passable for family events but not for a professional interview. Built-in mics pick up the electronic clicks and whirs of the equipment and are sensitive to any hand contact.

Don't use wireless mics for interviews unless you plan to spend the big bucks. Inexpensive wireless mics can pick up frequency interference from a host of sources such as cell phones, TV stations, CD players, computers, and PDAs. Your best bet for interviews is to use a lapel mic or shotgun mic mounted on a stand. This will ensure better sound quality because the mic can be placed close to the subject.

2. Not eliminating background noise.

Nothing spoils an interview more than background noise. You need to have the ears of a bat to eliminate unwanted sounds.

Make certain to turn off or unplug everything that you've control over. This includes heating and cooling systems, refrigerators and freezers, radios and music players, cell and landline telephones, and ticking clocks. Also make sure to close outside windows and the door to the interview room.

Before starting the interview put on your headphones and listen carefully for any stray background noise. If you've done your job thoroughly, all you should hear is the faint breathing of your subject.

3. Not using headphones.

If you're not wearing headphones, you can't adequately monitor the quality of the audio you're recording. Over-the-ear headphones are the best. Spend some money and invest in a good pair. Failing that, anything is better than nothing. Even the earbuds from your iPod will do in a pinch.

4. Recording with automatic gain control.

Unfortunately, most consumer video and audio recorders come with Automatic Gain Control or AGC. While it's easier to record sound, it also produces poor quality. The problem is that the gain control monitors the loudness or quietness of what you're recording and automatically adjusts the level. For example, when the interviewee pauses, the AGC raises the recording level, which in turn causes an increase in the ambient sound. When the person begins talking again the recording level is lowered. This produces a pulsing effect with the ambient sound that's difficult to eliminate without time consuming sound editing.

Do yourself a favor and spend enough to purchase a recorder that has a manual gain control. It'll mean monitoring your audio input continually, but you'll end up with good sound.

5. Failing to eliminate electronic hum and buzz.

Electromagnetic radiation or EMR is produced by such devices as power cables, computer monitors, radios, and TVs. Placing your video or audio recorder and audio cables next to these EMR sources can result in an audible hum or buzz.

Make sure that all your recording equipment is separated as far as possible from these EMR sources. Even a few inches can make a difference. If that's not possible, try crossing your power cable at right angles to your mic cables.

The bottom line: Don't push the record button until you've done everything possible to ensure that your audio will be pristine.

31 5 Reasons You Should Consider a Video Life Story

Most people when they consider a life story project think of a book. There are a lot of good reasons for producing a book. But I'll be honest. I have a video bias because producing video personal histories is my specialty. I also produce books but video is my passion. So why should you consider a video for your or someone else's personal history? Here are five good reasons.

1. Video conveys the emotional content of a story.

Watching someone choke up over a sad memory or laugh heartily at an embarrassing childhood moment powerfully captures a person's innermost feelings.

2. Video shows a person's special little traits.

One of the great strengths of video is that you can see and hear the person being interviewed. We are reminded of their uniqueness by the twinkle in their eye, their infectious smile, or their easy laugh.

3. Video harnesses a rich array of media elements.

Videos weave together interviews, photos, family movies, archival stock footage, music, sound effects, and graphics to produce a seamless and rich tapestry of an individual's life.

4. Videos are highly portable and easily duplicated.

A DVD weighs ounces and can be shipped inexpensively anywhere in the world. Now with a high-speed connection you can send your video to someone through the Internet. DVDs can also be easily and inexpensively duplicated.

5. Videos appeal to a media-savvy younger audience.

Your children and your children's children have grown up with computers, videos, and text messaging. If you want to get them to sit down with a family member's life story, chances are they'll watch a sixty-minute video before they'll read a lengthy book.

32 How to Set Up a Video Personal History Business

Are you thinking of setting up a video personal history business? A reader of mine is doing just that and asked for some advice. What I've learned over the past 30 years as a documentary filmmaker and personal historian might be of some value. So here goes:

Do...

1. Decide how much of the total production and post-production you're going to take on. Are you going to operate the camera and do the interviews? Or will these be separate functions? I do both and it works but it takes confidence in both your camera and interviewing skills.

Who will edit your raw footage? If you're going to do the editing, it'll require editing software and sufficient computer power to do the job. If you've never edited video before, it's a very steep learning curve.

2. Talk to other video personal historians who've been in the business for a few years. Most personal historians are happy to provide advice to newcomers. And each will have a slightly different perspective. You can find video personal historians by going to the Association of Personal Historians website (http://www.personalhistorians.org/) and clicking on the "Find a Personal Historian" button.

3. Determine the range of products you're going to offer. A full video life story with photos, music, graphics, and archival footage is expensive. Not everyone will be able to afford this. What can you offer that's less expensive? In my case I offer straight unedited interviews. These can be done quickly and because of this are relatively inexpensive.

4. *Do have a sample of your work.* Clients want to know that you're capable of excellent work. Put a sample on your website or have a video clip available for screening when visiting a client.

5. *Purchase the minimum amount of equipment necessary.* Camera, sound, lighting, and editing equipment is expensive. I've shot major television series for the National Film Board of Canada, using only one prosumer camcorder, one light, two lavaliere microphones, and a tripod. And I've continued using the same modest kit for my personal history business.

The reality is that you don't know if you're going to be successful or for that matter even enjoy the work. By starting small you minimize your financial risk. Down the road, if business is good and you love what you're doing, you can always upgrade your equipment

Don't...

1. *Don't buy overly expensive equipment.* This advice follows on the last point above. You can get a quite decent professional camcorder for under $3,000. For a single light you can get something under $600.

Good sound is important so the exception to my buy "cheap" rule is don't skimp on mics. I've been very happy with my Tram TR50 mics that are priced at $310 at B&H. If you want to save some bucks on a tripod and lighting stand, see what you can find on Craigslist or Ebay.

2. Don't forget to account for equipment depreciation. Unfortunately, your camcorder will be outdated the moment you leave the store. Chances are that within three years you'll be looking at the need to purchase a new model. That's why you want to build an "equipment rental" fee into your client's project costs. This can go toward the replacement of old equipment.

3. Don't let clients screen their video until the final cut stage. Most clients aren't familiar with the editing process. If they see a rough cut, they'll be alarmed and make suggestions, some of which will not be useful.

By showing them a fine cut, your clients will have a good sense of the video's content and flow. And if concerns arise, you'll still be able to make some editing changes without too much grief.

33 6 Top Sites for Free Online Videography Training

If video personal histories appeal to you but your experience with video production is limited, help is just a click away! You'll find a wealth of valuable resources in these six sites.

- Videomaker (http://www.videomaker.com/): "This is the place to start for videography training. Here you will find hundreds of articles about audio/video software, video editing hardware, and help with video lighting techniques."

- Video 101 (http://www.video101course.com/): "Offers tutorials on the fundamentals of film and video production. Includes video clips, flash animations, and explanations."

- BBC Academy (http://www.bbc.co.uk/academy): "Do you need to shoot a sequence and are not quite sure where to start? Have you shot unusable material and are not sure why? Learn from experienced program makers and use tools & guides to help you on your next shoot."

- VideoUniversity (http://www.videouniversity.com/): "Hundreds of free articles for new and advanced videographers. Here's a sample: 50 Ways To Improve Your Video Business; Video Art—An Introduction; Audio for Video—Tape Formats and Hardware; Audio For Video—Microphones & Techniques; Audio For Video—Audio Production Techniques."

- MediaCollege (http://www.mediacollege.com/): "... a free educational website for all forms of electronic media. We have hundreds of exclusive tutorials covering video & television production, audio work, photography, graphics, web design and more."

- Vimeo Video School (http://vimeo.com/videoschool): "...a fun place for anyone to learn how to make better videos. Start by browsing our Vimeo Lessons, or find specific video tutorials created by other members."

34 The Secret to Creating an Engaging Video Life Story

What makes a video biography memorable? Is it the person being interviewed? Or is it the inclusion of archival photos and movies? Or could it be the clever use of audio and visual effects? All of these are significant but the most important factor—the #1 secret to a first rate video biography is good storytelling.

Basically your video biography needs to have the same narrative structure that goes into creating a good feature film—pacing, suspense, and character development. It's true that your production isn't for broadcast and will only be seen by your client's family and friends. But that's no excuse to make it boring!

Here are a few ways you can improve your storytelling.

Launch your story with a compelling opening.

And I don't mean flashy effects (see more at Stop With the Effects! (36). That's window dressing. A good feature film captivates you in the first few minutes of the story. Edit a clip from the main interview that establishes your subject's character. It might be something that's funny, heavy with portent, sad, or revealing. Cut that into your opening. Later decide what visuals (e.g. family photos, home movies, etc.) you might want to accompany this opening segment.

Keep the story moving.

It's not enough to string together the chronology of a life. You need to use techniques that will give the narrative energy and create momentum.

One approach is to shift the emotional tone. For example, after your subject has recounted a sad story, fade to black and then come up on an account that's happy. Or if your subject has been railing at the world, jump to a tender story. Trust me, it works.

Another way to keep the story moving is to create a jump in time. This can improve your storytelling immeasurably by eliminating material that's lackluster.

For example, the story of a woman who struggles to get an education during the Depression and eventually goes on to university is riveting. But her university years are less interesting. What's really intriguing is how she gets her first job after graduating. So find a clip from her interview that can be used to jump directly to her first job. It might be something she says like, "I had great fun at university but it was my first job that really tested me."

Create suspense.

Suspense is the principal engine that drives your story.

Suspense is created by your audience asking and getting answers to such basic questions as, "What is the subject's quest? How does the subject resolve the challenges along the way? Will the subject reach a goal? What happens when the dream is achieved or not achieved?"

Here's the bad news. Unless you've asked these questions in your interviews you'll likely have little to help you create suspense.

Keep your editing tight.

As Sheila Curran Bernard, an Emmy and Peabody Award-winning writer, said, "In documentary, as in drama, you have to collapse real time into its essence."

Believe me, not everything your subject says is worth including in your video. Eliminate anything that doesn't support your main story.

For example, an anecdote about "Aunt Flo" might be interesting but unless it somehow illuminates some facet of your main subject, Aunt Flo should go! To give you some perspective on this, I shoot an average of six to seven hours of interview for a one-hour video biography.

Provide a good closing.

Your ending should provide a satisfying resolution to the central journey. It must be short and not introduce any new story lines. The final scene can be in the form of a simple summary statement from your subject. Or it can be some end cards that bring the story up-to-date. Whatever you choose, don't make the mistake of creating multiple endings.

35 9 Common Mistakes to Avoid When Using Your Camcorder

For those of you who are new to doing video interviews for a life story, here are some common mistakes to avoid.

1. *Failure to read the manual.* First and foremost know how to use your camcorder. Read the manual. Practice, practice, practice. And then practice some more!

2. *Failure to use the color balance.* Don't want blue or green looking skin? Learn how to set the color balance, which will improve your picture color.

3. *Dead batteries.* Make certain your batteries are fully charged and that you have an additional back-up battery.

4. *Failure to check electrical outlets for AC hum.* If you're using an electrical outlet to power your camcorder, check to make certain that you're not getting an electric "hum" on your audio.

5. *Dirty lens.* Nothing mars a picture more than a spot or smudge. Always clean your camera lens with a lens cleaning solution and lens tissue.

6. *Out of focus.* Check to make sure your subject is in focus. Use the manual focus rather than the auto focus.

7. *Incorrect exposure.* Make certain to check your exposure so that your subject is neither over nor under exposed.

8. *Incorrect Recording Mode.* You can choose from SP (standard play) and LP (long play). Use SP mode. It allows for downloading to a computer and provides a better picture.

9. *Failure to monitor audio quality.* Use a good quality lavaliere microphone if your camcorder has an external mic terminal. If it doesn't, then make sure that you place the camera no more than 4 feet from your subject. Also try to record in a room that is quiet, one with rugs, drapery, and padded furniture.

36 Stop With the Effects!

Have you noticed an annoying trend? Every videographer from "Cousin Harry" in Saskatoon to the BBC in London is causing our eyes and ears to bleed with cranked-up sound and tightly edited, over-the-top visual effects.

Today, even the simplest home editing software has a myriad of "bells and whistles." You can use the "Ken Burns" effect to pan or zoom in and out of photos. You can have dazzling titles and credits not to mention fancy dissolves and fades.

Now I'm not against effects. Don't get me wrong. I use them myself. Applied judiciously to enhance a story, they can be valuable tools. The problem arises when they're overused and distract you from the story being told.

I've watched many a video ruined by a filmmaker adding endless ramped-up motion to their photos. After a while I want to shout out, "For God's sake stop with all the motion! I'm getting seasick!" Nothing spells amateurish more than the overuse of visual effects.

Life story videos are not rock videos (unless of course you're producing Bryan Adams's life story). The effects should work with the subject being documented. We don't need MTV "razzle-dazzle." What we need are well-edited sequences that tell a compelling story with a beginning, middle, and end. We want to see pathos and joy, gravity and humor. We want, as with a good feature film, to be entertained.

If you're about to begin editing a video biography, stop! Keep your hands off the effects buttons. Only when you've got a strong storyline in place—only then—consider using effects. Think of them as the icing on the cake.

Maybe, if we're lucky, we can begin a movement back to thoughtful, elegant storytelling. And maybe my ears and eyes will stop bleeding.

37 Warning: Using Copyrighted Music Without Permission Is Illegal

Some of you may be unaware that including favorite pieces of music in your travel, birthday, wedding or life story videos is illegal if that music has a copyright. It doesn't matter if the only people who are going to see your production are family and friends. It doesn't matter if you've bought the CD and are using only a few clips. It doesn't matter if you're never likely to get caught. The truth is that using someone's original work and not paying for it is essentially stealing.

So what's the solution? You can get permission to use the music from the copyright holder. This is not for the faint-hearted. It can be a lengthy and expensive task—hardly something you'd want to do for Uncle Jack's retirement video.

There are several other possibilities. What I do is hire a local musician to compose and play original music for my videos. He's excellent and has been kind enough to give me a great rate. There are all kinds of struggling young musicians out there who would love to compose and play something that would work in your video. Check out your local music school, university fine arts department and the Internet.

Another solution is to use royalty free music available from a number of web-based companies. One I discovered and would certainly recommend is incompetech (http://tinyurl.com/8s4exle). Its owner/composer/musician Kevin MacLeod offers a wide selection of his own work and makes it available for free or a modest $5 donation. You can't beat that.

I've assembled a partial list of other royalty free music providers below. I haven't used any of these, so I can't personally vouch for them.

- Music 2 Hues (http://www.music2hues.com/)
- Sound Ideas (http://www.sound-ideas.com/)
- RoyaltFreeMusic.com (http://www.royaltyfreemusic.com/)
- 2 b Royalty Free (http://www.2b-royaltyfree.com/)

38 How to Avoid Landmines When Producing Video Ethical Wills

A reader recently asked, "Two people have consented to an ethical will but I think videotaping them would be more personal for the receiving family. Can you see some possible landmines?" This was my reply.

There are several things to be cautious about when undertaking a video ethical will.

- First, ensure that your clients prefer a video to an audio or printed ethical will. Some people suffering from a terminal illness don't want their families to have a lasting image of their decline.

- Will you have your clients speak directly to the camera or to you off screen? While speaking directly to camera can be effective for an intimate presentation like this, it can be intimidating for someone not used to facing a camera.

- Preparing an ethical will requires a good deal of reflection. Your clients will need time—perhaps a week or more—to fashion responses to the questions posed by an ethical will. I would suggest that, if at all possible, have them work on writing down their thoughts before actually videotaping their responses.

- Avoid having your clients rehearse their responses. This sounds like a contradiction of my previous point but it's not. You want people to have given sufficient thought to their ethical will but you don't want them to become fretful about getting it "right." This will end up producing results that are stiff and not natural.

- Be aware that you may unlock some painful memories. How comfortable are you with sadness, tears, and anguish? Do you have a counselor you can recommend to your client should things become more than you can handle?
- Above all don't rush the process. It takes time.

CHAPTER 7:

More About Digital Media

39 Act Now to Save and Store Your Old Photos

If you're like me, you've inherited old photo albums with the pictures held down on so-called magnetic pages. The trouble with these albums is that the adhesive used and the plastic liners damage the photos over time. Removing the photos is a priority. I went looking for help and boiled my research down to these seven essential steps.

Step 1

Before attempting any photo removal make certain to digitally scan each album page so that should a photo be damaged, you can still recover it from the scanned image.

Step 2

Select a practice photo that has no value to you or is badly out of focus. A word of caution: when removing photos. Be sure not to curl or peel them back as this could cause permanent damage.

Step 3

Use a piece of dental floss and carefully pull it under one corner of the photo. Using a sawing motion slowly work your way to the opposite corner. With any luck the photo should pop right off.

Step 4

If a photo is glued so tightly that floss won't work, then try one of the following removal methods:

  a. Use un-do, an adhesive remover that won't harm photos. It comes with an applicator that allows you to slip the remover under the photo.

  b. Place the album page in your freezer for a few minutes. The glue will become brittle, making it easier to remove the photo.

  c. Use a hair dryer set on low heat. Run it back and forth on the back of the page holding the photo. Be careful not to overheat the photo as this could damage it. Once the glue has softened, quickly and carefully remove the picture.

  d. Place the photo album page in a microwave. Make certain there are no metallic pieces. Start the microwave and run it for five seconds. Check the photo and keep using five-second blasts until the glue softens and the photo comes free.

Step 5

Take your photos and where possible write on the back the following information: the names of people in the photo, their ages, the year, the location, and the event. Avoid using a ballpoint pen as this could damage the photo. Use a soft lead pencil or an acid free pen available from a craft store.

Step 6

Digitally scan your photos, store them on your hard drive, and then upload them to a web based site like Flickr or Picasa. That way if your hard drive crashes, you won't lose your digitized photos.

Step 7

Store the original photos in cardboard photo boxes that pass the Photographic Activity Test (PAT). You can obtain such boxes at Archival Methods, Carr McLean, Light Impressions, Gaylord, and University Products. If you have a large collection, layer an acid-free sheet of paper between each photo. Photos should be kept in a cool room with low humidity. That generally means keeping them out of attics and basements.

40 7 Key Questions to Ask Before Transferring Your Video Tapes to DVD

When I wrote about the importance of protecting your family media treasures (see 39: Act Now to Save and Store Your Old Photos, I stressed the need to transfer your films and videotapes to a digital format. You can do this yourself if you have the equipment but if you don't, there are numerous service providers who can help you.

The problem arises when you try to decide how to choose the right company. Should you go with a local company or a large national chain? Does a more expensive service necessarily mean a better final product? Here are the seven key questions you need to ask a transfer service before agreeing to leave your videotapes and films with them.

1. What video and film formats do you accept?

The more professional the company the more likely they'll be able to handle a wide range of formats including the following: VHS, S-VHS, VHS-C, Video8, Hi8, Digital8, MiniDV, and Betamax in either NTSC (North American standard) or PAL. The most common film formats are 8mm, Super8 or 16mm.

2. How will my original tapes be returned to me?

It's scary shipping off your treasures. The last thing you want is for them to be lost in the postal system. Use a reputable courier service to deliver your videos to the transfer facility. And ensure that they will return your videos by courier as well.

3. How many hours of video can I get on one DVD?

Commercial DVD movies are made by an expensive process that involves preparing a glass master and pressing multiple DVD copies. A less costly process that uses a laser to burn information on a DVD-R disk is what consumer transfer facilities use. To maintain a high quality image you shouldn't put more than 90 to 120 minutes on one DVD-R.

Avoid any company that tells you that they can put more than that on a DVD-R disk.

4. Will my video look better when it's transferred to DVD?

The answer is no. Some larger facilities may be able to slightly enhance the original quality of the video. But if the image on your video is badly faded, there is no way to bring it back to life. Don't believe a company that tells you they can perform miracles.

5. Do you use professional video processing equipment?

If the answer is yes, the company should explain that they use a time base corrector, a detailer, and processing amplifier. This equipment will produce a better quality DVD than can be made on your home computer or at a "Mom and Pop" operation.

6. Do you have testimonials from satisfied customers?

Satisfied, happy customers are a good indicator of a well-run company. I always look for testimonials.

7. How long have you been in business?

I would tend to use a service that has been around for a few years and established a good reputation.

41 How to Protect Your Films, Videos, and Digital Media

According to the National Audio-Visual Conservation Center, the lifespan of consumer physical digital media is estimated to be five years or less.

Those family photos that you've stored on disk or the DVD of your last trip won't last forever either. So what to do? Here's what I'd suggest to protect your collection:

- Copy all of your film, audio and videotapes to a digital format.

- Keep alert to new formats and ensure that you copy all of your collection to the new format.

- Make certain all your audio and video tapes, old film stock and digital media are stored in a room that is free from dust and extreme fluctuations in temperature and humidity.

- Keep your collection away from direct sunlight and liquids. All audio and video tapes should be kept away from any magnetic fields and other electronic equipment.

- Store your media upright in rigid containers specifically designed for that particular media. Cardboard sleeves are not suitable for storage.

- Handle your discs by the outer edge or inside hole. Never grab them by the surface. The grease and salt from your fingers will damage the disc.

- Drives should be cleaned regularly to avoid damaging your tapes.

- Don't leave a tape in the drive of a recorder for a long period of time.

For further helpful information on preservation check out Independent Media Arts Preservation at http://www.imappreserve.org/pres_101/index.html#digital.

42 How to Salvage a Damaged Audiocassette

A personal history colleague of mine in Victoria inspired this article. She wondered if I knew anyone who could fix an audiocassette that no longer seemed to work in her recorder. I confessed that I didn't have any recommendations.

So I got to thinking, "How difficult is it to repair an audio cassette?" I did some research. Then I took apart a cassette and amazingly put it back together again! It requires patience and a steady hand but it's not an impossible job. A word of caution. Tapes that have melded from prolonged exposure to heat and humidity are not something you're likely to fix on your own. This will require a professional conservator and be a costly undertaking.

But if your problem is a tape that has become mangled inside its case or the cassette mechanism is broken, then here's what you can do. My advice would be to practice first on another tape before tackling the one you want to repair.

Broken cassette

1. Purchase a cassette shell from an A/V supplier or find a good cassette that you're no longer using. Open it up and remove the original tape.

2. Find a clean table and place your cassette flat with the screw side facing up.

3. Take a small Phillips screwdriver and carefully remove the five screws. Place them in a small container.

4. Carefully lift the top off, noting how the tape is threaded in the mechanism and the placement of the components.

5. Lift your tape out of the old shell and thread it carefully into the new one. Make sure to keep the tape untwisted.

6. Place the top back on the cassette, making sure that all the pieces fit and that nothing is pinched. Insert the screws and tighten.

Mangled tape

1. Open the cassette as described above and survey the damage.

2. If the tape is crinkled, just leave it. The sound may not be perfect but cutting out the offending piece or trying to smooth it out will only make the situation worse.

3. If the tape is broken, you can purchase a splicing kit or do it yourself with some sharp scissors or razor blade and Scotch tape. Not perfect but it'll work.

4. If the edges of the broken tape are ragged, trim just a fraction off each end. Remember that whatever you cut off will also cut out some of your recorded audio.

5. Cut a piece of Scotch tape exactly the width of your tape and about 3/8-inch long. Trim off any overhang. Failure to do this will cause the tape to stick to the internal mechanism.

6. Place half of the Scotch tape on one end of the audio tape and press it down firmly. Make sure your tape is straight. If it isn't, the tape will run unevenly and may be damaged further. Now attach the other half of the Scotch tape to the remaining half of audiotape making sure to form a seamless joint. Don't overlap the ends. Press down firmly on this remaining segment.

7. Carefully rethread your tape and seal up the cassette as described above.

8. One final word. Once you've made your repairs, plan to transfer your tape to a digital format as soon as possible. You can find out how to do that at lifehacker (http://tinyurl.com/mvcslj.

CHAPTER 8:

Writing and Editing

43 Book or Video? Which Makes a Better Personal History?

It's fair to say that most clients think of a life story in book form rather than video. That's why I wrote 5 Reasons You Should Consider a Video Life Story (31) where I extolled the virtues of video. As I said, I have a bias because my background is in documentary filmmaking. But I've also produced several books. So which is better? Each format has its strengths and weaknesses. You be the judge. Here are six areas where books triumph over videos.

1. Books will last.

Printed on archival paper and properly stored, books will be around longer than any current digital media. The best "guesstimate" for DVDs is a lifespan that ranges from 5 years to over 100 years depending on the manufacturing process of the DVD and its storage. But the bottom line is that no one knows for certain.

2. Print books don't require hardware to be read.

Digital hardware and formats continue to change. There's a thriving business in transferring old media to current formats. Who out there doesn't have a box of old videotapes waiting to be digitized? But you can still pick up a book printed a century ago and read it.

3. Books capture detail.

Books are splendid at documenting the intricacies and depth of a story. This isn't video's strength. Video prefers a broader stroke and emotional content over detail.

4. Books have presence.

You can hold a book in your hand. It has weight, texture, and odor. It almost demands that you pay attention. A DVD case, no matter how attractive the labeling, feels insubstantial.

5. Books are convenient.

You don't have to plug them in, recharge batteries, or worry about dropping them. You can pick up a book and in an instant start reading.

6. Books are accessible.

An attractive life story book set out on a coffee table invites friends and family to pick it up. There's no need to set up equipment to view it.

How many of you provide your potential clients with a choice of a book or video personal history? Do you think you should?

44 Editing Brings Out the Gold

Many of my potential clients aren't familiar with how a book or video life story is actually produced. They're often quite surprised at the number of hours it takes to do a professional editing job. Over the years I've tried to explain the editing process using analogies that might create an "Aha" moment for my clients.

If you're reading this as someone who's interested in having your or someone else's life story told, perhaps my analogies will help you understand the process. If you're a personal historian, these examples might be something you can add to your bag of tools.

The cabinet maker analogy:

Editing is like making a fine piece of furniture. Let's say you want an end table built. The cabinet maker you hire starts with the raw material, usually hardwood. She carefully measures and cuts the pieces according to a blueprint. The pieces are then assembled but at this point the table is still rough and requires sanding. The final stage involves using finer and finer grades of sandpaper until the table is ready for varnishing. Layers of varnish are laid down and rubbed smooth between each application.

The result is an exquisite heirloom quality end table you'd be proud to display in your home. So too the print or video editor starts with the raw material of the interviews. After cutting them down and structuring the story she polishes the manuscript or video by refining the initial edit and then working on an attractive overall design.

The gold panning analogy:

I got this analogy from reading an interview with Studs Terkel, the famous American oral historian. He said that editing was like a miner panning for gold. The miner had to carefully sift through earth and gravel before he came up with some flecks of gold in the bottom of his pan. Like the miner, Terkel said he had to go through the transcripts patiently extracting the gems that were locked away in the interviews. It was a long and painstaking process.

The symphony orchestra analogy:

Editing is similar to composing a symphony. There are many different instruments, each with its own unique qualities and sounds. It's not enough simply to write down a bunch of notes and hope that somehow a beautiful sound will be produced. You have to structure each section of the symphony so that when it is played it not only has a beginning, middle, and end but that it is harmonious and polished.

Like a symphony composer, the editor pares away at the raw interview material and shapes it so that it has structure and no extraneous notes and is beautiful to read.

45 9 Editing Tips to Turn Your Transcripts Into Gold

In producing a book on someone's life story, the work of recording the interviews is just the beginning of the creative process. You'll need to make transcripts of the interviews and then edit them.

Editing transcripts makes the story come alive. By removing the extraneous words and tangled syntax and structuring the transcript into a coherent and interesting narrative, you'll strike gold.

Here are nine tips that will help you with your editing.

Tone and style:

Make sure to keep the "voice" of the person you're editing. Don't rewrite the interview to the point where it sounds like you!

Repeated words:

Watch out for words and phrases that are repeated. Readers will become bored.

Sentence length:

Vary the length of sentences. Alternating long with short sentences makes it easier and more natural to read the completed story. As a rule, the shorter the sentence, the more energy it gives the writing. Research shows that twenty-word sentences are fairly clear to most readers. Thirty-word sentences are not.

Adverbs:

People tend to use adverbs to give emphasis. The result is the opposite. All words ending in "ly" should be used sparingly.

Commas:

People don't speak with commas in mind so you will have to place them in your edited transcript. Many phrases, compound sentences, and most modifying clauses call for commas. Commas make a sentence comprehensible to the reader.

Eliminate "just" and "so":

Whenever you encounter these words, drop them. They're not needed.

Vary the first word:

Try to make the first word of each paragraph as well as the first word of every sentence different from the one before.

Compress and clarify:

Think hard about every word you use. Is it necessary? Is there a concise way to say this? Follow the rule of one idea per sentence.

Logical order:

The story needs to be written so that the reader can easily follow the narrative. Where does the story begin? What's in the main body? And how does it end?

46 10 Indispensable Self-Editing Books

Whether you're a novice or a seasoned professional, these ten reference books are a must for your library. My thanks to the following Association of Personal Historians colleagues who suggested many of these books: Pat McNees, Mim Eisenberg, Stephen Evans, and Philip Sherwood.

1. *Write It Right: The Ground Rules for Self-Editing Like the Pros.* "In a succinct five-step process, this reference shows how to save time and frustration when editing one's own work, creating stronger, more precise text that holds the reader's attention. Through its practical, field-tested approach featuring frequently asked questions and key points for reflection at each step, writers learn how to avoid embarrassing themselves on paper, remain objective throughout the process, pinpoint their own unique writing challenges, and recognize when it is time to call for outside help. Tips and examples in the grammar and usage section further illustrate how to overcome the most common writing challenges that plague writers."

2. *The Savvy Self-Editing Book.* "... a guide for writers to develop their own editing process to suit their needs and vision. It breaks down the editing process into three stages: Content, Sentence, and Copy Editing. Its concise format gives writers concrete examples, charts, and quick and easy editing techniques that make a difference."

3. *Editing Fact and Fiction: A Concise Guide to Book Editing.* "From the job descriptions of editorial staff members through the minutiae of the actual editing process, ...[the authors] cover this field thoroughly and with astonishing concision."

4. *The Copyeditor's Handbook: A Guide for Book Publishing and Corporate Communications.* "...lively, practical manual for newcomers to publishing and for experienced editors who want to fine-tune their skills or broaden their understanding of the craft. Addressed to copyeditors in book publishing and corporate communications, this thoughtful handbook explains what

copyeditors do, what they look for when they edit a manuscript, and how they develop the editorial judgment needed to make sound decisions."

5. *Line by Line: How to Edit Your Own Writing.* "…over 700 examples of original and edited sentences, this book provides information about editing techniques, grammar, and usage for every writer from the student to the published author."

6. *The Fine Art of Copyediting.* "This well-crafted book focuses on the details of copyediting and as a bonus gives advice on human relationships in the editorial process. Well-written, insightful, concise, and punchy, this compact book provides a novice with the basics of copyediting and is a useful and fun review for old hands…" ~ Reader Review

7. *On Writing Well.* "… belongs on any shelf of serious reference works for writers." ~ New York Times

8. *Edit Yourself.* "As a professional editor, I rely on many tools. I consistently return to Ross-Larson's book because it is thorough while being easy to use. I can find what I want fast. I particularly like his list of word substitutes: after reading "in addition to" and "in view of the fact that" a hundred times, I forget the simple substitutes. Ross-Larson's book consistently brings me out of the engineering woods." ~ Reader Review

9. *The Artful Edit.* "Susan Bell, a veteran book editor, also offers strategic tips and exercises for self-editing and a series of remarkable interviews, taking us into the studios of successful authors such as Michael Ondaatje and Ann Patchett to learn from their various approaches to revision. Much more than a manual,

The Artful Edit inspires readers to think about both the discipline and the creativity of editing and how it can enhance their work."

10. *Grammatically Correct.* "For those who value correct grammar, Anne Stilman has written the definitive guide. She holds you to her high grammatical standards, and clearly explains how to follow the rules. There are chapters on "Spelling," "Punctuation," "Grammar," and "Style," and Stilman patiently elucidates the rules of colons, brackets, and plural formations, while gracefully tackling the common misuses of "lie" versus "lay.""

47 How Much Detail Should a Life Story Contain?

That's the question some of my colleagues at the Association of Personal Historians have examined.

Some feel that details count because they can enrich a life story by providing a social history context for it. They suggest that what might be tedious to the interviewer could in fact be fascinating to family members now and in the future.

Other personal historians see a need to be selective with details, choosing only those that enhance a story—sifting out the chaff and creating a more readable and entertaining narrative.

But the debate about how much detail to include is better settled after thinking through the following questions:

Is this a book or video life story?

In Book or Video? Which Makes a Better Personal History (43), I extolled the strengths and weaknesses of both print and video. Books are more suited to detail than video. Video's strength is in storytelling, broad strokes, and emotional content.

What's the budget?

If you want detail, it's going to take time and time costs money. Ten or more hours of interview isn't uncommon for a full life story. While your client might want their very own version of *Gone with the Wind,* their budget restrictions point to a more modest affair like *Swayed by the Breeze.* ;-)

How open and revealing is your storyteller?

Some people need little prompting to unleash a wealth of detailed stories. Others are more reticent. No matter how sensitive and clever your questions, you're lucky to get the bare bones of the person's life.

What kind of questions are you asking?

The interview is at the core of a comprehensive and entertaining personal history. If you want to get the stories behind a life, avoid questions that focus exclusively on names, dates, and places. Instead, use open-ended questions that begin with How, Where, When, What, and occasionally, Why. And don't read from a series of scripted questions. Make sure to go deeper with prompts like "And then what happened?"

Conclusion

I believe that details can enrich a life story. Ultimately though, we're hired as professionals to edit and weave those details into a coherent and engaging story.

48 Are Those Memories Really Accurate?

It seems that the way our brains store and recollect memories is kind of quirky. Our brains frequently convert rumors, falsities and opinions into perceived, recollected fact, says Scott LaFee in an article in the *San Diego Union-Tribune.*

"Everybody does it," said Sam Wang, an associate professor of molecular biology and neuroscience at Princeton University. "Memory formation and retrieval isn't like writing something down on a piece of paper. Memories drift and change, and things we may have once doubted, we no longer do."

As we recall stored facts, said Wang, our brains reprocess them, collate them with new information, re-interpret the result, then re-store them as new and "improved" memories.

What does that mean for those of us writing our own or our client's memoir? I think what we need to keep in mind is that we want to render a three dimensional portrait—not fret about getting every little detail correct. What's important is that it's your story, your recollections, and your response to the events in your life. If a brother or sister saw things differently, so what? It's not their story.

What I aim for in producing a life story for my clients is something more than just a chronological retelling of the events in their lives. I want to know how they responded to events; how they felt; the life lessons they learned; the values and passions that have driven them; their triumphs and tragedies and their hopes and dreams.

So, don't worry. Like me and everyone else, our past memories are most likely an amalgam of fact and fiction. What's really important is that we start recording and preserving memories now before they're lost forever.

49 How to Engage Your Readers

In a nutshell—show, don't tell.

Here's an example taken from my own life:

Telling: "In September 1966 I left for a two year assignment as a volunteer in Ghana."

Showing: "I still remember that 'muggy' September night at Mirabelle airport in Montreal. It was 1966 and I was hours away from leaving Canada for the first time in my life. I couldn't sit still. As I paced about the departure lounge, I felt a mixture of excitement and apprehension. For the next two years I would be a volunteer teacher in an isolated rural secondary school in Ghana, West Africa. My youthful bravado said I could handle it. My more rational mind questioned my confidence."

The "telling" example is a simple statement of fact. It lacks any emotional content. It's flat and not engaging. By contrast, the "showing" example is rich with detail. We know it was humid and hot in Montreal. And we know something of what I was feeling and what was on my mind. By showing readers what was happening rather than telling them, we draw them into the story.

If you're interviewing someone for their life story, the same rules apply. Bring out the emotion, flavor and detail of their story. If someone says, "I was married in 1939" enrich this statement by using some follow-up questions like these:

- What second thoughts did you have about your marriage?

- Describe the preparations that went into your wedding.

- What emotions were running through you on your wedding day? What stands out for you?

- Describe for me the place where you were married.

- What kind of weather did you have?

- What funny incident happened on your wedding day?

- Describe for me your wedding celebration.

- How did local or world events play into your wedding plans?

Here are some additional resources to help you with your memoir writing:

- *Writing the Memoir* by Judith Barrington. *The Library Journal* says, "Her practical guide leads both experienced and novice writers through the writing process from idea to publication, addressing such technical problems as theme selection, voice, tone, form, plot, scene, and character development, as well as how to stimulate creative thinking and build necessary discipline."

- *The Situation and the Story: The Art of Personal Narrative* by Vivian Gornick. *Publishers Weekly* says, "Gornick's book discusses ways of making nonfiction writing highly personal without being pathetically self-absorbed. In admirably plain and direct style, she discusses writers as diverse as Oscar Wilde, Joan Didion and a man she calls the "Jewish Joan Didion," Seymour Krim...All the texts do nevertheless support her statement that essays can "be read the way poems and novels are read, inside the same kind of context, the one that enlarges the relationship between life and literature."

- Memoir Mentor (http://www.memoirmentor.com/) is a terrific website for aspiring memoir writers. Dawn Thurston offers generous tips on improving your writing. She has also written a book with Morris Thurston entitled, *Breathe Life Into Your Life Story.* "Written for both novices and experienced writers, this book presents techniques used by novelists to immerse readers into their fictional world—techniques like "showing" rather than just "telling;" creating interesting, believable characters and settings; writing at the gut level; alternating scene and narrative; beginning with a bang; generating tension, and more."

50 How to Make the Weather Part of a Life Story

Weather plays a big part in our lives yet we often forget to include weather details when we sit down to write our personal history.

My mother vividly recalled how it was pouring rain when she got married in the tiny hamlet of Alert Bay, British Columbia.

I remember one Christmas when I was all of 8 years old. My family lived on an isolated island near the northwest tip of Vancouver Island. Rarely did we get snow at Christmas. That year it started snowing after supper on Christmas Eve. I was delighted and so excited that I stayed up all night looking out my bedroom window as my little part of the world turned white. It was one of my most memorable Christmases.

If you're interested in making weather a part of a life story, I've discovered a great resource. It's called the Weather Warehouse (http://weather-warehouse.com/index.html). You can get direct online access to the most comprehensive historical weather database in existence. It provides United States weather details going back as far as 1902.

You can also access international data offline starting from 1973. So let's say you wanted to know what the weather was like when "Aunt Beatrice" immigrated to New York on July 18, 1922, you can find out at Weather Warehouse. There is a charge for the service starting for as little as US $4.95.

51 How to Put "History" Into Your Personal History

Looking back on our lives or the lives of our family members, we can see that we've been eyewitnesses to many of the world's great events. For example, during the Great Depression my father rode the rails looking for work. My mother flew in some of the first regularly scheduled airline flights. I knew exactly where I was and what I was doing when I heard of President John Kennedy's assassination. And we can all remember vividly our gut reaction on seeing the collapse of the World Trade Center on September 11, 2001.

One of the invaluable legacies that our personal stories provide is not only a record of our lives but also an oral history of our times. Don't forget to weave into your narrative important historical events and how your client reacted to them. I would give anything to hear my grandfather's firsthand account of the battle for Vimy Ridge during the First World War. It was a defining moment in that war and a defining moment in Canada's coming of age as a nation.

Several websites offer some excellent "Today in History" information. If you want to find out what was happening on a birthday or what world events occurred on a wedding day, then check out these sites:

- BBC's On This Day (http://news.bbc.co.uk/onthisday/default.stm)
- The New York Times On This Day
  (http://www.nytimes.com/learning/general/onthisday/index.html)

- History.com This Day In History (http://www.history.com/this-day-in-history.do)

52 Bringing the Dead to Life: Writing a Biography of an Ancestor

The other day I was asked if I had any ideas about writing the biography of a dead family member. This struck a responsive chord in me. For some time I've wanted to write about my mother's father, my grandfather. He was only thirty-two when he died in 1920. A Winnipeg fire fighter, he succumbed to the great flu pandemic that was sweeping the world. My mother was only two when he died and she had few stories about him.

Maybe you're also thinking about writing the life story of a distant family member. Before beginning, you'll need to pull together as much information as you can on your ancestor. Here's an approach I'm going to use for my grandfather's story. You might want to try this.

Locate relatives and friends.

Where possible, audio record interviews with descendants. Try to find out as much as you can, whether it's first person accounts, documents, or leads to other people who may have information about your relative.

Research documents.

Personal letters, diaries, and wills, as well as census, land, church, probate, and court records, may yield details of your subject's life. For example, I've contacted The Fire Fighters Museum of Winnipeg (http://www.winnipegfiremuseum.ca/home.htm) to ascertain if there are any records of my grandfather.

Search for historical and cultural information.

This will give you some clues about your relative's life. In my case, I want to find out about the working life of Winnipeg fire fighters around 1920. What were the qualifications to get into the fire department? What did the job pay? How many hours a day did they work? Was there a pension plan?

Read local and ethnic histories.

These can provide clues as to how your relative may have lived and provide interesting texture to your story. For example, I want to read newspaper accounts of the impact the flu pandemic was having on Winnipeg.

53 How to End Your Book or Video Life Story

The questions which one asks oneself begin, at least, to illuminate the world, and become one's key to the experience of others. ~ James A. Baldwin

Imagine that you're coming to the last chapter of a book or the final hour of a video life story you're doing. It may be your own or it could be a story you've been hired to record. Every detail has been covered from childhood to the present. How can you wrap up this life story in a way that feels satisfying? As a colleague said, "The book is ending; the life is not."

An approach of mine that you might try is to use the final chapter to explore what I call contemplative questions. These are questions that go to a person's core values and beliefs—such things as life lessons learned, regrets and successes, hopes for the future, expressions of forgiveness and gratitude, and spirituality.

While some of this content may arise naturally in the course of recounting a life, it's useful to focus on it at the end of the interview process. Why? Because as a personal historian I find that my clients and I have developed a rapport by the end of hours of interviewing. There is a level of trust and comfort that is more conducive to sharing heartfelt convictions.

Another reason for covering this material at the end is that by that point a person has looked back on their life and examined it in detail. This process of recollection naturally begins to raise existential questions.

One lesson I've learned though, is that these contemplative questions should never be sprung on people. The first time I tried this, my poor client stared at me like a deer caught in the headlights. People need time to reflect and compose their answers in a calm and unhurried manner. Now I hand out the contemplative questions to my clients a week or two in advance so they have time to think them over.

There's no right way to end a life story. But if you're searching for an approach that works, I'd recommend using a series of contemplative questions. You can find a sample of contemplative questions in another article, Life Stories and Palliative Care: Your Questions Answered (77).

54 4 Reasons Why You Need to Hire a Book Designer

You know a design is good when you want to lick it. ~ Steve Jobs

We all love good design. That's why the iPod and Ikea have been so successful. Design is the difference between something that is OK and something that is memorable. If you hope to have a successful personal history business producing books, you'll want to include a designer on your team. Here are four important benefits of good design.

Good design affects people emotionally.

You'll lose clients if your books have great content but look homemade. When prospective clients see your work, they don't have time to read the content. They'll be primarily influenced by how attractive the books look. Advances in neuroscience have shown that people tend to act first on emotion, then follow it with reasoning to support their choice. The more people are emotionally drawn to your work, the more likely they'll hire you.

Good design conveys credibility.

Don Norman, a former Apple design guru, sees the value of producing good design. He says, "We all have the feeling that attractive things work better." If you produce first-class books, your company projects quality, care, and professionalism.

Good design supports and enhances the content.

It's true that content is vital. But if you have to struggle to read a book, you're not likely to enjoy it. We can all recall coping with a poorly designed book with type that's too small or inappropriate for the subject, no white space for the text to breath, lack of headings to provide guidance, and photos placed without any seeming logic. Remember that in addition to your client, others will read your book. Your books are your calling card. They speak in your absence. Will your books speak of quality and great design?

Good design differentiates you from the others.

It's becoming a crowded field in the world of self-publishing. A compelling design will set you apart from all the others.

55 My 50-Second Rant!

I seldom rant. I don't like ranting. It seems somehow boorish and annoying. When I do rant it has to be for a good cause. So forewarned here's my 50-second rant!

I've recently encountered some people who feel that when it comes to a life story of a loved one, the final product needn't look attractive. "I'll just take the pages down to Kinko, have them copied and stapled together. That's good enough. People will just toss them in a drawer anyway." Someone else told me, "I'll just get a friend to make copies of these DVDs. No need to worry about labeling or boxing them."

Why is it that people will spend days pouring over the renovation design for their kitchen and yet give hardly a thought to what a legacy book or video will look like? Marshall McLuhan, the Canadian communications theorist said, "The medium is the message." He was absolutely right. If we give people a book or video that looks like crap, then that's how people will perceive the contents.

Surely, we owe the ones we love the honor of presenting as beautiful a memoir as we can provide. It should be an heirloom that will be cherished and handed down from generation to generation.

That's it. That's my rant. I feel better now.

56 6 First-Class Short Run Printers

Are you looking for a reliable, quality, short run printer? These six all come highly recommended by my colleagues at the Association of Personal Historians.

I haven't used any of these printers and can't vouch for them. So make sure to use due diligence before making a selection.

Bookmobile

"In 2010 a book is no longer just a book. A book is a paperback, a hardcover, or, of course, an ebook. It needs to be in the form the reader wants it, when the reader wants it. As a publisher you see opportunity in this epochal change. At BookMobile, we see the vision we created in the '90s being realized."

Custom Museum Publishing

"Custom Museum Publishing specializes in the creative design, production and printing of full-color books, exhibit catalogs and marketing materials for artists, galleries, museums and historical societies. Located in beautiful mid-coast Maine, our newest printing technology makes your showcase-quality products affordable in either small or large quantities. In addition to perfect-bound and hardbound books and exhibit catalogs, we offer calendars, note cards, post cards, brochures, and large-format signage. We also offer experienced exhibit photography and copy editing."

Family Heritage Publishers

"Utah Bookbinding Company is the binding division of Family Heritage Publishers. It has been in continuous operation since its establishment in March 1952. It has been owned and operated by the same family since the beginning. It is the premiere library binding company serving the Intermountain West. Its experience is unsurpassed in the industry with employees having a collective experience of over 100 years."

First Choice Books

"Book publishers, small publishing presses and independent authors who wish to self-publish will find our self-publishing company affordable, trustworthy and dependable. Quotations are provided within 2 to 3 business days and a hardcopy proof within 2 weeks. Our high tech book printing equipment and experienced, friendly team of professionals will make your publishing experience enjoyable and informative."

Friesen's

"'Our company will be successful only if our customers are successful.' Those were the words of D.W. Friesen who started our company in 1907, in Altona, Manitoba. What started as a small confectionery store has grown to become one of Canada's leading independent companies, specializing in book manufacturing and printing."

Gorham Printing

"We are a Pacific Northwest book printer specializing in book design and book printing for self-published books. At Gorham Printing, it's easy to turn your manuscript into a professional quality book. If you are looking for exceptional book design combined with quality book printing, you've come to the right place!"

57 Warning: The Perils of Self-Publishing

The New York Times Sunday Book Review ran an article, "You're an Author? Me Too!" about the phenomenal growth of published works. In 2007, 400,000 books were published or distributed in the United States, an increase of 100,000 from the previous year. The industry tracker Bowker attributes this incredible rise to the number of print-on-demand books and reprints of out-of-print titles. Self-publishing companies would tend to support this assessment. IUniverse, a self-publishing company established in 1999, has grown 30 percent a year and now publishes 500 titles a month.

With print-on-demand making it easy and relatively inexpensive to publish, should you be looking at your life story as the next best seller? The evidence, despite a few exceptions, shows that self-published books sell few copies.

The *Wall Street Journal* wrote a cautionary tale about the pitfalls of self-publishing. It told the story of C. Ben Bosah, an environmental engineer, who thought his wife's health book was a sure-fire best seller. He ordered 15,389 books and at the time the article was written had sold less than half.

But let's say you're not convinced of the perils of self-publishing. You know that you've got a winner on your hands. What I'd suggest is that before you do anything, run to your library and pick up the following books recommended by Pat McNees, a colleague in the Association of Personal Historians. These books are some of the best and will give you a clear-eyed view of what's required to promote and market your book. Good luck!

- *1001 Ways to Market Your Books,* Sixth Edition
- *Beyond the Bookstore: How to Sell More Books Profitably to Non-Bookstore Markets*
- *Complete Guide to Self Publishing: Everything You Need to Know to Write, Publish, Promote, and Sell Your Own Book*

CHAPTER 9:

Workshops

58 7 Things You Can Do to Ensure a Great Workshop

Workshops are an excellent way of getting yourself in front of potential clients. Running workshops is something I really enjoy. Over the years I've learned a few things about designing and facilitating them that I'd like to share with you. Here are seven things you can do to create an optimum learning environment for your workshop.

1. Set up a comfortable workshop space.

Nothing does more to kill a good workshop experience than a poorly lit room that is too hot or too cold, too big or too small. Ask for a room that will comfortably hold the number of participants. Avoid having chairs lined up with military precision. Request a U-shaped seating pattern if that's possible. This provides for greater intimacy and participation.

Finally, always arrive early to check out your room and make certain it's set up to your specifications.

2. Greet participants when they arrive.

I always make a point of welcoming participants and giving them a folder of workshop resources. This creates a friendly, inclusive atmosphere and allows you to get a quick sense of who's attending your workshop.

3. Avoid telling participants what they already know.

Remember that your workshop participants are a tremendous resource from which to draw. Adult learners bring a wealth of experience. Start with the assumption that your participants already have some experience and ideas about the topic.

4. Check out expectations.

This flows from the point above. One way to find out what people want to learn is to ask them! Somewhere near the beginning of my sessions I make a point of asking people for their workshop expectations.

5. Build in participatory activities.

Avoid lecturing. If you must, keep it short—like five minutes! People enjoy being involved. How many activities you can do will depend on the size of your group and the length of your workshop. If the group is small (fewer than twenty participants) use pairs or triads to get people engaged with one another. For example, in determining expectations, I divide the group into pairs. I ask each person in the pair to describe to the other what it is they most want to learn. After about five minutes I bring everyone back to the group and solicit their expectations. Then I write these on a flip chart.

6. Create a safe and comfortable learning experience.

Your workshop participants will, for the most part, be strangers to one another. They need to feel comfortable with each other before speaking up in the group. That's why I design ways to get people into smaller clusters that allow participants to get to know one another more easily.

7. Lead by example.

Your words, body language, and tone should read relaxed, attentive, non-judgmental, supportive, and open. I often start my sessions by saying, "In our workshop today no one gets to be wrong...including me!" I emphasize that all questions are legitimate and will be listened to respectfully.

59 How to Make Your Life Story Workshop Memorable

I always use some short, entertaining exercises to help break the ice and add a little fun and variety to my life story workshops. If you're looking for something, consider some of those on my list.

The six-word memoir.

Made popular by Smith Magazine, the idea of the six-word memoir is to have participants use only six words to capture their life stories. I usually hand out small 2x3-inch cards for people to use. After some sharing of mini memoirs, I collect the cards and put them in a box for a prize drawing at the end of my workshop.

The story behind my name.

I divide the class into pairs if it's large and have each partner share the story behind his or her name. After about 15 minutes I gather the group together and have people share their "name" stories. It's always a crowd pleaser!

A favorite object.

Everyone has something they treasure. I bring a favorite item of mine to the workshop. I talk about what it is, how I acquired it, and why it's special to me. Then I have the class break into pairs and have each partner describe a favorite object. After 15 or 20 minutes, I ask for some sharing of "favorite object" stories.

A peak life experience.

I describe to the class a peak moment in my life. I provide as much detail as possible – where it was, when it happened, who was there, and how I felt. I then have the workshop participants find a partner and have each share with one another a peak experience. After 15 to 20 minutes, I have the group reassemble and ask for volunteers to share a peak moment.

A special place.

This can be from any period in one's life. I recall a huge hollowed out tree stump in the forest near our home. This was my special place when I was a boy. It was off the beaten track and known only to me. I would go there when I was feeling adventurous or when I was troubled. I ask my workshop participants to share with a partner a special place in their lives. Later I ask for some individuals to share a description of a special place.

A photo story.

I'll admit that I haven't tried this exercise yet. I dreamed it up recently and can't wait to use it in my next workshop. I have a photo from my personal collection that I'll use. Here's the exercise. I'll hand out a copy of the photo to workshop participants and ask them to take 20 minutes to write a story behind the photo. I won't give any clues as to the real story. Then I'll ask various people to read out their stories. I think there'll probably be some interesting variety. To conclude I'll tell the real story of the photo.

60 More About the "Mini Memoir"

An exercise I particularly like to use in workshops is the six-word memoir. This is based on Smith Magazine and their popular six-word collections.

The idea is rumored to have started with Ernest Hemingway. He was challenged to write a six-word story and he wrote:

Baby shoes for sale, never worn.

I think the six-word memoir is a great way to get your creative writing juices flowing. Having trouble starting your life story? Why not write a six-word memoir and use it as the title for your book. Alternatively, turn it into the introduction to your story. These mini memoirs can be intriguing and often call out for a fuller explanation.

To give you some inspiration, here are a few of the six-word gems from the participants in a previous workshop of mine.

- Mom's revenge, I am my mom!
- Who said it couldn't be done?
- I'm aching, broken but I'm alive!
- Work hard. Live well. Enjoy life.
- Waiting to see what is next.
- Daughter, sister, wife, mother, grandma, wow!
- Have motorcycle, will travel. I'm free!
- Family is my Love and Joy.
- Love it all. Not enough time.
- Years happen. Still learning. Constantly amazed!
- Investing in others now. Rewards coming.

Here is mine: Learned much. Much more to learn.

What's your six-word memoir?

CHAPTER 10:

Ethical Wills

61 Ethical Wills Part I: How to Begin

Writing your ethical will is about reflection. It's about taking the time to sit back and really reflect on who you are. Now some of you may have had plenty of time to do that already. Others of you may find it hard to squeeze yet one more thing into a busy day. Not to worry. When I wrote my ethical will I was so busy my "hair was on fire." Believe me, if I could do it then you can do it now. Here's how I'd suggest you begin.

Ask yourself why you're writing an ethical will and for whom.

It's important. Otherwise it's too easy to say, "Ah, this is too much trouble. I'll start on it some other day." Chances are you'll never get back to it. In my case I wanted to write an ethical will for my partner. I wanted not only to talk about the things that mattered in my life but what I was grateful for in our years together. In the event that I died, I wanted to leave behind a legacy letter that would be of some comfort—a letter from my heart to my partner's heart. I also found it useful to have someone in mind to whom I was writing rather than a generic, "Dear family" or "Dear children" approach. So, let me ask you why you're doing this? Is it to share with your spouse things about you that aren't always self-evident? Or do you want to offer some life lessons to your children that may serve as a guide as they grow older? Perhaps you're writing your ethical will for a long trusted friend? Please note. Ethical wills are not the place to get even with someone or to sermonize on how someone else should lead their life. Those are poison-pen letters!

Buy an inexpensive lined notebook.

The notebook will become your workspace as you develop the content of your ethical will. Now I can hear some of you saying, "Pen and paper! What's wrong with using my computer?" Remember what I said at the beginning. This is an exercise in reflection. It helps to disconnect ourselves from all the electronic devices that whir and click and ping. For many of us, workdays are spent staring at a screen. Finding a quiet corner undisturbed by a flickering computer screen will go a long way toward allowing your mind to relax and be reflective.

Write the opening lines of your ethical will. At the top of the first page of your notebook write, "Dear..............., I'm writing you this ethical will because............" If you've done steps one and two this should be relatively simple.

Schedule a regular time to work on your ethical will.

To make certain you maintain some momentum and get your ethical will written, block out some time. Think of a time of day when it's relatively quiet—a time when you're most reflective. For me it's early in the morning. Mark into your calendar at least 30 minutes, three times a week. If you can do more, that's even better. The important thing is to make a date with yourself and stick to it.

Good luck in getting started!

62 Ethical Wills Part II: Discovering Our Values

What are values? The American Heritage Dictionary describes a value as: "A principle, standard, or quality considered worthwhile or desirable." And believe it or not, Elvis Presley said, "Values are like fingerprints. Nobody's are the same, but you leave 'em all over everything you do."

I like to think of values as a part of our DNA. For each person they are unique. They explain what motivates us, what angers us, what we cherish. Knowing our values gives us a clue as to who we are. Our values develop over time and are shaped by our parents, teachers, community and religious affiliation.

So how do we uncover our real values? Let's start with three simple exercises. These are not meant to tell you what your values should be. They simply provide a way to discover what your values are.

Exercise one:

Open your ethical will notebook that you started. Leave a few blank pages from the first page where you wrote your introduction. These will be the pages on which you'll write the final draft of your ethical will. After these few blank pages write the heading, "My Values."

Think of a best friend and the qualities you admire in that person. For me, the qualities I admire in my friend are loyalty, humor, dedication, fairness, and honesty. Now take a moment and write down the qualities you admire in your friend. As you look at your list, ask yourself, "Would these qualities describe me as well?" Chances are most of them would. And why? Because we make friends with people who tend to share the same values as ourselves.

Exercise two:

Ask yourself, "What are some things that really tick me off?" For me, pomposity, impoliteness, and arrogance get me pretty steamed. So what are the things that can really upset you? Take a moment to write down your list. Within this list you'll find good clues to some important values you hold. When a value that's important to us gets stepped on or violated it upsets us. Let me illustrate using my own example. Pomposity goes against my value of unpretentiousness. Impoliteness violates my value of politeness, and arrogance assaults my value of humbleness.

Try this next exercise to unearth some more of your values.

Exercise three:

Write down at least three things that give you real pleasure and joy. For example, for me that would be:

- Discovering new things and learning new stuff.

- Witnessing a magnificent sunset.

- Seeing a dear friend after a long absence.

What are some of the things that bring you pleasure? After you've compiled your list, take a look at each item and see if you can pull out some of the underlying values. For example, my pleasure in discovering new things and learning new stuff taps into my values of learning and exploration. My joy at seeing a beautiful sunset links to my values of beauty and spirituality. And seeing an old friend connects with my valuing friendship.

By now you should be developing a pretty good list of some of your core values.

If you want to explore this topic in more depth consider these books: *What Matters Most: The Power of Living Your Values* and *Values Clarification.*

You may want to reflect on your list and see if other values come to mind. Perhaps there are some important values that you have missed in your list. Remember these are your personal values—not your parents' or your society's.

The next step.

Put your values into a sentence that will become a part of your ethical will. Using myself as an example, I'd take my values recorded above and write, "Some of the values that have guided me over the years have been loyalty, humor, dedication, fairness, honesty, unpretentiousness, politeness, humbleness, beauty, spirituality and friendship."

If you want to add some "meat" to your list try taking one or two of your most cherished values and recount a personal story that illustrates how these values were put to use in your life. If you need some inspirational guidance check out *This I Believe: The Personal Philosophies of Remarkable Men and Women.*

63 Ethical Wills Part III: Expressing Gratitude

Why bother including gratitude in your ethical will? Here are several good reasons:

- Research indicates feelings of gratitude may be beneficial to our emotional well-being (Emmons & McCullough, 2003)

- Expressing gratitude to another provides a moment of grace and joy for that person.

- Academic studies indicate that grateful people are on the whole less materialistic than the general population and tend to suffer less anxiety about status or accumulating possessions.

Preparing your ethical will is a wonderful opportunity to reflect on what you've been given by others. And examining in detail all that you've been given generates a natural feeling of gratitude. So, let's begin work on this week's ethical will exercise.

SKILLS FOR PERSONAL HISTORIANS

Exercise: Take your ethical will notebook and turn to the next available blank page. At the top write the heading "Gratitude." The notes you write here will eventually become part of your final ethical will draft.

Now write the following sentence. "What I have received from…(insert the name of the person to whom you're writing your ethical will)..is…."

Here's an example. Writing of my mother I said, "What I have received from my mom is her unconditional love, her support and encouragement when I needed it, the importance of politeness, consideration, and grace, and the value of loyalty."

What are the things that you've received? When you've compiled your notes, take time to go back and for each item expand upon it so that it's phrased as an expression of gratitude. Keep in mind that when you write about gratitude it's best if you explain a specific incident that illustrates why you're grateful.

Example. Continuing with my mom I wrote, "I'm ever grateful for your support and encouragement when I've needed it. When I was beginning my career as a documentary filmmaker many years ago, you were not only one of my early "fans" but you also came to my financial rescue on several occasions. Without your support I know I may never have succeeded."

The idea is to provide substance and detail to your expressions of gratitude. Don't just say, "I'm grateful for your love." Rather, say something like, "I'm grateful for your love. I know that there are days when I'm too exhausted from work to feel much like talking. You've always been sensitive to that and given me the space I need. Thank you for that. It has meant so much."

You may want to continue your exploration of gratitude and discover the benefits that can accrue to you. One suggestion is to keep a "Gratitude Journal." At the end of each day write down at least five things you're grateful for that day. I find it's also useful to add a reason after each thing you're grateful for. For example, "I'm grateful for the comfortable bed I sleep on because so many are homeless and sleep on the street." And here's an important point. The things you're grateful for don't have to be "earth shattering." They can be simple things that make your life worthwhile....like a comfortable bed.

Robert A. Emmons, professor of psychology at the University of California, Davis, is one of the foremost authorities on the topic of gratitude in North America. He has said,

> *... it's important to stress that gratitude is really a choice. It doesn't depend upon circumstances or genetic wiring or something that we don't have control over. It really becomes an attitude that we can choose that makes life better for ourselves and for other people... When things go well, gratitude enables us to savor things going well. When things go poorly, gratitude enables us to get over those situations and to realize they are temporary.*

You might find these two books by Emmons useful additions to your library: *Thanks!: How the New Science of Gratitude Can Make You Happier* and *Words of Gratitude for Mind, Body, and Soul.*

64 Ethical Wills Part IV: Life Lessons Learned

An important aspect of an ethical will is being able to share with others the life lessons we've learned over the years. Why is this important?

To begin with it's useful to reflect on how much wisdom we've actually gained from our experiences. Some of our most profound insights come from the so-called "bad" events in our lives.

For me, at the tender age of twelve, I lost my dear dog, Mickey. It was a devastating event. We had been inseparable. From that and from the loss of another dear friend years later, I eventually learned that nothing remains constant. Everything changes, and no matter how intensely we may love others, it cannot stop the inevitable—their deaths.

Today, a life lesson I know from experience is that we must live and love each day as if it may be our last.

Sharing our life lessons with others permits them to understand what guides us. And I think it's also a way for people to begin to reflect on their own lessons learned. For the young, our ethical will can provide a living example of the power of life experiences to teach us wisdom.

Exercise: Turn to a blank page in your ethical will notebook and at the top write, "Life Lessons." Now use each of the following prompts below to write down your lessons learned.

Some of these may not apply to you. Skip those and move on to the next. Remember that you'll eventually transfer your notes to the front of your notebook when you finalize your ethical will at the end of the series. As with my personal example above, try to give the background story to a lesson you've learned.

- From my father I've learned....
- From my mother I've learned....
- From my favorite teacher I've learned....
- From my best friend I've learned....
- From my work life I've learned....
- From my (partner, spouse) I've learned....
- From my children I've learned....
- From my brother I've learned....
- From my sister I've learned....
- From my neighbor I've learned....
- From my cat I've learned....
- From my dog I've learned....
- From old age I've learned...
- What I've learned from failure is....
- What I've learned from success is....
- What I've learned from my faith is....

SKILLS FOR PERSONAL HISTORIANS

65 Ethical Wills Part V: Expressing Forgiveness

All of the world's major faiths include forgiveness as a principle tenet.

- **Buddhism:** To understand everything is to forgive everything. *(Buddha)*

- **Christianity:** Be kind and compassionate to one another, forgiving each other, just as in Christ God forgave you." *(Ephesians 4:32)*

- **Islam:** Keep to forgiveness, and enjoin kindness. *(Qur'an 7:199-200)*

- **Judaism:** When asked by an offender for forgiveness, one should forgive with a sincere mind and a willing spirit...forgiveness is natural to the seed of Israel. *(w:Mishneh Torah, w:Teshuvah 2:10)*

Implicit in these admonitions is the realization that an important foundation of a healthy individual and society is an avoidance of anger and revenge. Today's medical researchers are also discovering that forgiveness has positive health benefits. Katherine M. Piderman, Ph.D., staff chaplain at Mayo Clinic, Rochester, Minnesota, lists thirteen benefits from practicing forgiveness.

1. Lower blood pressure

2. Stress reduction

3. Less hostility

4. Better anger management skills

5. Lower heart rate

6. Lower risk of alcohol or substance abuse

7. Fewer depression symptoms

8. Fewer anxiety symptoms

9. Reduction in chronic pain

10. More friendships

11. Healthier relationships

12. Greater religious or spiritual well-being

13. Improved psychological well-being

It's important to remember that forgiveness is not forgetting or condoning bad behavior. You may never be able to forget someone's unwarranted actions. But forgiveness can release you from the grip of resentment and thoughts of revenge.

An ethical will is a place where you can not only forgive others; you also can ask forgiveness for hurtful actions on your part. Forgiveness is not easy. It is a slow process that begins by reflecting on how a particular action has made you feel and your commitment to work toward forgiveness.

Exercise One: Take your ethical will notebook and turn to a blank page. At the top write "Forgiveness." It may strengthen your "forgiveness muscle" by doing a little warm up exercising. For the next seven days, at the end of each day, write down a list of incidents that you'll forgive. They can be trivial or serious. And don't forget to forgive yourself for mistakes you might make.

Here's a sample list:

Day One –

- I forgive the driver that tailgated me.

- I forgive the rude clerk in the grocery store.

- I forgive myself for being late for an appointment.

- I forgive my friend for forgetting my birthday.

As you write down each of your forgiveness items, take a deep breath. As you exhale let go of any lingering anger or judgment. Remind yourself that the past has passed. Focus on the present, knowing that clinging to old grievances will do nothing but keep you unhappy.

Exercise two: Make a list of all the times you can think of where you have wronged various people in your life. Now at the bottom of your list write the following, "I'm not perfect. I make mistakes. With the wisdom of hindsight I would have behaved differently. That was the past. Now I forgive myself for my actions and move on."

Exercise three: Take time to reflect on the years you've known the person to whom you're writing your ethical will. Recall any incidents where you still harbor some grievance towards that person for something that was done to you. Now write the following, "With all my heart I want to express my forgiveness for the time when……." For example, "With all my heart I want to express my forgiveness for the time when you challenged my decision to leave my corporate job and become self-employed."

As well as giving forgiveness you may wish to seek forgiveness from this same individual. Again think of times when you may have wronged that person. Now write, "Please forgive me for the time(s) when…….." For example, "Please forgive me for the times when I've not acknowledged your help with my parents. I'm truly sorry."

Check out the following books for more help.

- *Forgive for Good* by Dr. Fred Luskin
- *Forgive and Forget* by Lewis B. Smedes
- *The Art of Forgiveness, Lovingkindness and Peace* by Jack Kornfield

66 Ethical Wills Part VI: Regrets, Achievements, and Hopes

In Part Six you have an opportunity to look back and reflect on the regrets and achievements in your life. After that we'll focus on your hopes for the future and the hopes you have for those you love.

Regrets

Writing about regrets can help you understand the circumstances that led to the regret and hopefully provide you with some insight. Regrets are inevitable—but take some comfort in knowing that we've all made some major blunders in our life, so you're not alone.

In his book *No Regrets*, Dr. Hamilton Beazley, lists 10 steps to letting go of regrets and the very first step is to write them down.

Exercise: In your ethical will notebook, find a blank page and at the top write the heading "Regrets." As you look back on your life, make a list of your regrets. Don't worry if some are seemingly insignificant—put them down anyway. For example, one of my regrets is that I never learned to swim. Now this isn't huge and if I really wanted to, I could enroll in a swimming class for adults. What's important is that you just begin the process of listing regrets.

Look at your list and select one or two regrets that you consider to be significant. Write about this regret and what you've learned and attempt to put it in some perspective. As an example, in my ethical will I wrote,

> *One of my regrets in life is that I never pursued my belief that I had the potential to be a television or radio host. I'm a natural in front of an audience and my publicity appearances on TV and radio have always been fun. I loved the energy involved. What I know though is that had I pursued that avenue so many other doors would have been closed. I would never have made the films I have and most likely wouldn't be a personal historian, something I truly love. Besides, if I still have the "bug" I can find avenues to satisfy my interest. Who knows, maybe I'll host a Community Radio or Television program on "Life after 50."*

Achievements

The Miriam-Webster Dictionary defines achievement as a result gained by effort. The result can be big or small. It's the effort that counts. What I want you to consider in this section are your achievements. Our lives may have been filled with prominent achievements or unheralded ones. This is an opportunity to write about what you consider important. My mother believed her main achievements were running a well-organized home, being a loving wife and mother, and producing the best pastries in the neighborhood.

Exercise: Turn to another blank page in your notebook and write the heading, "Achievements." To help you reflect on your most important achievements, try answering this question: If you were to be honored for one thing in your life, what would it be? Another way of looking at achievements is to look at what you hope your obituary will one day say about you.

Hopes

One of my favorite quotes about hope is by American writer Barbara Kingsolver. "The very least you can do in your life is to figure out what you hope for. And the most you can do is live inside that hope."

Exercise: Find a blank page in your ethical will notebook and at the top write, "Hopes." What is it that you hope for? How have you lived inside your hope? What do you hope for your loved ones?

Some books you might find helpful:

- *Woulda, Coulda, Shoulda: Overcoming Regrets, Mistakes, and Missed Opportunities*
- *Finding Hope: Ways to See Life in a Brighter Light*
- *Maximum Achievement: Strategies and Skills That Will Unlock Your Hidden Powers to Succeed*

67 Ethical Wills Part VII: Putting It All Together

If you've been working on your ethical will, you'll have filled up a good many pages in your notebook. Now it's time to put it all together.

Here's what I'd suggest you do:

- Read each section (Beginning, Values, Gratitude, Life lessons, Forgiveness, Regrets, Achievements, Hopes) from the beginning to the end and add any thoughts or comments that you might have missed the first time around. You may have some "Final Thoughts" that you wish to include.

- Look at some sample ethical wills and get some ideas of how other people have composed their ethical will.

- Write out a first draft of your ethical will that incorporates the material you've assembled in your notebook over the last six weeks. Don't try to sound "profound." Just write the way you talk. And remember that there is no "right way" to put your ethical will together. It's your document and should reflect who you are as much as possible.

- Now read aloud your ethical will and rewrite anything you stumble over.

- Once you're happy with your composition, find some good quality archival paper and acid free ink. This will ensure the preservation of your document.

- In your best handwriting, copy from your last draft a final version of your ethical will. Even if you've been using a computer up until now, I can't stress enough how much more valuable your ethical will be if it's written in your own hand.

- At this point you have a number of options with your completed ethical will. You can keep it locked away, to be given to the recipient after your death. You can deliver it by post or in person now. Or you can read it to the recipient before handing it over. The choice is up to you.

CHAPTER 11:

Working with Clients
at the End of Life

68 How Life Stories Can Benefit the Dying

Over the past 15 years I've had the opportunity to be involved with people at the end of their lives, first as a documentary filmmaker and more recently as a personal historian and hospice volunteer.

What I have learned from firsthand experience and the growing body of academic research is that telling life stories can have a therapeutic effect on the dying. The process of recording and preserving life stories provides the terminally ill with:

- *Affirmation.* By recording patients' stories you are acknowledging that they encompass more than their illness. They are people who have lived and in living have experienced what it means to be human.

- *Legacy.* Patients are aware that their life stories will transcend their death. There's hope that they will be remembered and that their stories will provide some comfort to families in their bereavement.

- *Purpose.* Patients feel that by doing this work there is still meaning to their lives. At the end of life when so much of an individual's independence and contribution is restricted, regaining a sense of purpose is invaluable.

- *Pattern.* When people have an opportunity to look over the span of their lives they see more clearly a purpose and meaning to experiences that often seemed random and discontinuous.

- *Support.* Having care providers, friends, family members, or personal historians listen to patients' life stories bears witness to who they are and the significance of their journey.

For any of you working with palliative care patients or caring for a dying family member, I strongly encourage you to consider introducing some life story activity into your care.

69 Questions to Consider Before Offering a Personal History Service to the Terminally Ill

I know some of you are interested in the possibility of providing personal history services to the terminally ill. I've been helping those at the end of life record their personal histories as well as volunteering at Victoria Hospice for the past five years. I find it tremendously satisfying work but it's not for everyone. If you're seriously contemplating working with the dying, here are seven questions to ponder.

1. How flexible are you with your schedule?

If you're someone who gets easily frustrated and cranky when your plans go awry, then this may not be the work for you. People who are ill can plan to meet you on a certain day but at the last moment cancel because they're not feeling up to it. Or they simply forgot because medications can sometimes make people a little muddled. At other times family or friends drop by unexpectedly and you're put on hold. You have to accommodate ill people's schedules, not yours.

2. How calm are you?

Terminally ill people are already under a lot of stress. They don't need you to add to it. If you're a high-energy Type A personality, easily flustered, who finds it hard to sit still, then this isn't the work for you. When you're with people who are dying, you need to be able to set aside your own problems and mental shopping lists, and be focused, present, and relaxed.

3. How patient are you?

This is a big one. There's always something that can go wrong. If you're an impatient person, you'll not last long at this work. Circumstances can alter dramatically. As I mentioned, schedules can change abruptly. Or you're told on arrival that everything recorded on the previous visit must be deleted because people fear it may be offensive to their family. Or you arrive at the same time that "home care" arrives to start vacuuming the house. Sometimes you find that you had scheduled an hour-long interview but after fifteen minutes people are too tired to continue. This is after you've driven thirty minutes or more to get to the patient's home.

4. How comfortable are you around sadness?

Being with people who are near life's end is inherently sad. Your interviews will naturally unlock tears in people as they're reminded of their shortness of time. And it's sad when you've come to know someone well and that person dies. If you are by nature a melancholy person, or one who avoids emotionally challenging situations, this is not the work for you.

5. How well do you deal with disappointment?

If you're someone who needs concrete accomplishments and goals, you might be disappointed by this work. Sometimes a life story is abruptly terminated because the person you're working with becomes too ill to continue. You're left with a half-completed story with no chance of finishing it. Or stories you know would be invaluable to the family are "off limits" because people don't want to talk about anything that might make them "tear up."

6. How good are you at establishing boundaries?

As you spend time with terminally ill people, your role as a professional personal historian may become compromised. Let me be clear. Your work doesn't involve running errands, counseling, being friends, or providing help with physical care.

You must be clear about your boundaries. It may be appropriate occasionally to pick up some item on your way over for an interview but you're not a delivery service. You're definitely not a therapist and you shouldn't be offering anything that remotely appears to be counseling.

Spending time talking to people about their lives is by its very nature intimate work. Occasionally you may sense a budding friendship. This is a tough one to handle. Think carefully what a friendship will involve. Are you able to spend the time and emotional energy that such a relationship will entail? My advice is to move cautiously on this one. As far as any kind of physical care, such as helping with a transfer or feeding, don't do it! You are not a health care professional and you could cause your subject serious injury.

7. How do you handle stress?

Providing personal history services for those at end-of-life is stressful. Whether it's meditation, a hobby, long walks, or visits with friends, you'll need to do something to manage your stress. If you don't have ways of coping with stress, then you'll become burned out by this work.

70 How Prepared Are You to Interview Terminally Ill Clients?

Life continually challenges us with the unexpected. And only a fool would attempt to prepare for the unforeseen. It does help though to go into uncharted territory with our eyes open to potential risks.

Now imagine yourself in the following situation. You're interviewing an 80-year-old woman, Rose, who lives with her daughter, Sandra. The daughter provides much of the caregiving. Rose suffers from a number of heart-related problems.

This is your third visit. The daughter tells you that she'll be out doing errands while you spend the next hour interviewing her mother. Sandra assures you she'll be back within the hour. It's just you and Rose alone in the house.

About halfway through the interview Rose develops severe pains in her chest. She asks you to hurry and get her nitro pills in the kitchen. You find a tray with numerous medications but nothing labeled nitro.

Back in the living room you explain this to Rose. She suggests you call her daughter whose cell phone number is on a message board in the kitchen. But when you try to find the number, it's nowhere to be found.

Rose is becoming increasingly agitated and calls out to bring the tray of medication to her in the living room. A number of questions race through your head.

- What if she picks the wrong medication with calamitous results?
- If something goes wrong, what should I do?
- I'll have to leave soon for an urgent appointment and Sandra hasn't returned home. Should I leave anyway?
- What would you do?

As a general rule, it is vitally important that as a personal historian working with a terminally ill person, you don't begin to undertake caregiving tasks. You weren't hired for this and indeed may put yourself and your client at risk if you step into such a role.

Having said that, you could find yourself in a situation similar to the one described with Rose. And with no one available to help, you may have to step in.

There are a range of possible responses, none totally satisfactory. But here are some suggestions:

1. If Rose is registered with a local hospice, there may be a number you can call for just such a crisis. Someone there would have a list of her medications and be able to help you. If she isn't registered with Hospice, then go to step 2.

2. Assuming Rose is clear mentally, bring the tray and ask her to point to the nitro pills. Read out the name of the drug and ask if these are indeed the nitro pills. If she confirms they are, then allow her to select the bottle and take the prescribed dose. Don't select the bottle for her.

3. Stay by Rose's side and monitor her progress. If she shows signs of recovery, you can breathe easy. If her condition worsens, call 911.

4. Assuming all is well, you still have an urgent appointment to keep. Sandra, Rose's daughter, hasn't returned. And you feel uncomfortable leaving Rose on her own. Here's what you might do:

   - Ask Rose if there is a neighbor who could come over and stay until Sandra returns. If there is, contact the neighbor and have that person come over.

- If there's no one who can come over, I'd opt to stay until Sandra returns. As urgent as your appointment may be, it is not worth risking someone's safety. Call and re-schedule your appointment.

A final word. One way to avoid the kind of predicament I've described is to make certain that you're never alone with a person whose health is severely compromised. Don't allow a family caregiver to use you as a means to get out of the house. Pleasantly and firmly point out that your arrangement with your client doesn't involve caregiving responsibilities.

71 How to Interview Someone Who Is Terminally Ill

Over the years I've recorded the life stories of a number of terminally ill people. I'm also a hospice volunteer. I've learned some things through my work and hope these tips may be useful if you're working with someone gravely ill.

- Negotiate how much time your subject feels he/she can handle in any one interview.
- Carefully monitor the strength of your subject while conducting the interview. If you sense he/she is fading, ask if you should stop or continue.
- People at the end of life can't always be at their "charming best." If you find that you're sometimes met with sharpness or even anger, don't take it personally. It's not about you.

- Be calm and mindful with a terminally ill person even if you're not feeling calm and mindful.

- Time is of the essence. Cover the most important topics first. You may not have time to complete the whole story.

- If you can't find a quiet space and must be in a room with others, check with your subject about confidentiality. He/she may feel uncomfortable talking if others can listen in.

- Some medications can make people forgetful so make sure you know what material you've covered. You may need to remind your subject that he/she has already spoken on a particular topic.

- Your subject may have difficulty hearing. Remember to sit close— no more than 3 feet away—and to speak clearly and with sufficient volume to be heard.

- Be flexible. Don't be surprised if an interview session you've arranged has to be canceled at the last minute. A terminally ill patient's condition can change dramatically in a short period of time.

- Take care of yourself. Working with someone who is dying is emotionally draining. Make sure you do things that bring you nourishment and strength, such as listening to your favorite music, meditating, doing a vigorous workout, or taking a long relaxing bath.

- Before starting to work with someone who is dying, be clear what your own feelings and attitudes are around death and grief. Are you comfortable in the presence of someone who is dying? Are you able just to be with someone without trying to fix anything? If you haven't explored your own feelings, this might not be the kind of work you want to be doing.

- It is entirely possible that you may not be able to complete someone's life story before that person dies. How well do you handle situations for which there's no "tidy" wrap-up?

- Taking care of yourself is vitally important because of the stressful nature of the work. Have someone to talk to about your feelings. And by this I don't mean talking about the person you're interviewing. That should always be in confidence. What I mean is being able to express your sadness, fatigue, anger, loss, and frustration to someone who is compassionate and non-judgmental.

72 When Time Is Running Out, What Do You Focus On?

At Victoria Hospice we're into the fifth year of a Life Stories Service for patients registered with hospice. This is a program that I initiated and continue to be involved with as a trainer and a mentor for our Life Stories volunteer interviewers.

Among the concerns that have arisen for the interviewers, one, in particular, has been problematic. What part of a life story do you focus on when it appears patients may have only a few weeks or days to live? Patients may initially indicate that they want to talk about the broad spectrum of their lives from childhood to the present. The reality, unfortunately, is that they're not likely to have enough time to complete such an undertaking.

Here's what I've suggested. The hospice interviewer and patient agree to start with contemplative questions first. These are questions that reveal something of who the person is, rather than the details of their life. If time permits, they can always go back to talk about childhood beginnings and the important stories from their life. So what might some of these contemplative questions be? Here are some samples.

- What would you like to say to your loved ones?

- What has been important in your life?

- What are you the proudest of in your life?

- What do you admire most about each of your children?

- What has brought happiness to your life?

- What's the most valuable thing you've learned in life?

- What regrets do you have?

- How would you like to be remembered?

- What is it that most people don't know about you?

- What are you grateful for?

Even if you're not involved with palliative-care patients, you may find yourself at times interviewing someone who's very frail and elderly. There's no guarantee that time is on your side. In such cases you may want to give some thought as to what's essential to record. Focusing on more contemplative questions may be the answer.

73 Caution: End-of-Life Interviews May Unlock Traumatic Stories

There are benefits for patients in capturing the stories of their lives and conveying special messages to loved ones, but a word of caution. It can also be a time when traumatic incidents from a person's past can resurface. These could involve physical or sexual abuse, loss of a child, and so on. You're not likely to encounter such stories but it does happen. It's happened to me. What should you do if such a situation arises? Here are my suggestions.

Stop recording.

People can forget that their words are being recorded and will eventually be heard or read by family members. You must ask your subjects if this is information they want others to hear. If it is, then when you begin recording again you need to say on the recording that you have spoken to your subjects and they have expressed a wish to continue with this aspect of the story. If on the other hand they say no, then you will want to ensure that all references to the incident are removed from the recording.

Remember you're not a therapist.

It's important to remind yourself that your role is not to help mend people. You're there to facilitate the recording of a life story. However, it's wise to have the names of several trusted counselors that you can refer people to should the need arise. If your subjects are clearly distressed by past events, you can suggest that they might want to talk to a counselor.

Bear witness.

It's possible that your subjects don't need or want any therapeutic intervention. And they don't want this part of the story recorded. They may only want to relieve themselves of a terrible burden that perhaps no one knows about. Telling you, in confidence, is a way to bring some closure to a difficult episode in their lives. Listen and bear witness. Do not explore, suggest, or otherwise engage in any therapeutic activity. If you sense you're getting in well over your head, it's time to suggest to your subjects that they talk to a counselor.

74 Musical Memories Are the Last to Fade

According to a recent study at the University of California, listening to music can be of benefit to Alzheimer's patients. I became aware of this several years ago when I directed a series of documentary films for the National Film Board of Canada entitled *Caregivers*.

In my research I talked to a number of people caring for a family member with Alzheimer's. What was remarkable were the number of stories of people who had all but forgotten who they were but who could still sit down at a piano and play or sing songs from long ago.

The poet William Cowper in his poem *Music and Recollection* captures the power of music to unlock memories:

With easy force it opens all the cells

Where Memory slept. Wherever I have heard

A kindred melody, the scene recurs,

And with it all its pleasures and its pains.

Such comprehensive views the spirit takes,

That in a few short moments I retrace

(As in a map the voyager his course)

The windings of my way through many years.

The other day, I was again reminded of this phenomenon. I was responding to a colleague's request on the Association of Personal Historian's Listserv. She was asking for help on how to gather information for a life story from an individual whose memory was fading. I mentioned the possibility of using music to aid in memory recall. This sparked recollections from other Listserv members who reminisced about touching moments when music helped an aging parent. They have generously allowed me to share these stories with you here.

- My mom, Marie, died from Alzheimer's. She had always loved music and played the piano by ear. Shortly before she died, long after she really knew who we were, long after she could walk or take care of her basic needs or read or even carry on much of a conversation, my sister wheeled her over to the grand piano in the facility where she lived. And she played a tune. I had forgotten all about this until I read Dan's post. As they say, "thanks for the memories." ~ *Susan Owens, www.talesfortelling.com*

• I worked briefly on a project a few summers ago with a neighbor whose mother no longer remembered anyone in the family or her group of long-time friends (I was actually helping him wrap up her story because he had given up on getting more information).

While he was visiting her one day in a facility where she was staying after a fall, he watched as his mother drifted toward a member of another family. They had walked into the community room carrying a violin case for one of the other residents. Without hesitation, his mother rolled her wheelchair up to the stranger and asked if she could "see" the violin. And, to his amazement, moments later, she was playing it!

My neighbor, her son, knew that she had played in her younger years, before marrying, and that she had always said she was quite good. In talking with her after the impromptu concert, she suddenly asked if he would like to take lessons from her. He had no desire to learn but accepted her offer so that they would have a mutual activity.

Weeks later, she bragged about him as "her star pupil" and, during their breaks, she ended up telling him stories from a part of her life that he'd never known. The "lessons" lasted nearly a year before her mind and her physical control began fading rapidly. Interestingly, during those months, she became very introspective about her parents and the impact they had on her life and very philosophical about her aspirations and dreams – but, the observations and assumptions she made were based on the period of her life as a concert violinist!! ~ *Stephen Evans, www.the-freelance-editor.com*

• As we were moving my parents out of their home into an assisted living facility (because my dad needed that kind of care), one of the last things to leave the house was the old family piano. It had been in Dad's childhood home and he had played most evenings after supper for more than eighty years. The evening before the piano movers arrived, my partner Kathy and I went over to have dinner with my parents. Kathy, who is a very talented musician, went to the piano and began to play. Knowing that Dad loved Jerome Kern's melodies, she started out with some tunes from "Showboat." Dad had been sitting in his armchair, staring blankly at the wall. When the music began he suddenly focused on Kathy and started to sing along, perfectly on pitch, with every word of the lyrics intact. They played and sang together for almost two hours while Mom and I smiled at each other and wept silently in the other room. It was the first time that Dad had perked up like that in months, and it was a wonderful gift to us all. Dad wasn't able to play a single note by himself anymore, but with Kathy's help the music came back to him. ~ *Linda Coffin, www.historycrafters.com*

75 A Personal List of Books on Dying

Do you have an interest in recording the life stories of palliative care patients? If you do, I can tell you that it's very satisfying and rewarding work. Over the years I've had the honor and privilege of bearing witness to those who were dying. In the process I've accumulated a library of resource books that I've found particularly useful.

This is an eclectic selection and by no means exhaustive. However, you might find the list helpful if you're planning to work in this specialized area of personal histories.

Tuesdays with Morrie: An Old Man, a Young Man, and Life's Greatest Lesson (Mitch Albom, Broadway, 2002)
"This true story about the love between a spiritual mentor and his pupil has soared to the bestseller list for many reasons. For starters: it reminds us of the affection and gratitude that many of us still feel for the significant mentors of our past. It also plays out a fantasy many of us have entertained: what would it be like to look those people up again, tell them how much they meant to us, maybe even resume the mentorship?" From *Amazon.com* Review

Dying Well (Ira Byock. Riverhead Trade, 1998)
"Byock, president elect of the American Academy of Hospice and Palliative Care, is a gifted storyteller. Beginning with his own father's terminal illness, he details without scientific cant the process of decline that awaits most of us. The case studies, which form the humanistic soul of this work, never devolve into the maudlin or saccharine. Life on the edge of the great crossing is explored in all its sadness and pathos, but Byock also makes room for wisdom, hope and even the joy of final understanding." From *Publishers Weekly*

Another Morning: Voices of Truth and Hope from Mothers with Cancer
(Linda Blachman, Seal Press, 2006)

"Another Morning is the best oral history of the experience of cancer that I have ever seen. The women's voices are angry, sad, and most of all, loving, as they tell stories of illness, loss, families and motherhood. Linda Blachman has written an essential documentary resource for clinicians and health researchers, and she offers those living with cancer the companionship of generously shared experiences." Review by Arthur W. Frank, MD, author of *The Renewal of Generosity* and *The Wounded Storyteller*

Final Gifts: Understanding the Special Awareness, Needs, and Communications of the Dying (Maggie Callanan and Patricia Kelley, Bantam, 1997)

"Impressive insights into the experience of dying, offered by two hospice nurses with a gift for listening. The "final gifts" of the title are the comfort and enlightenment offered by the dying to those attending them, and in return, the peace and reassurance offered to the dying by those who hear their needs." From *Kirkus Reviews*

The Year of Magical Thinking (Joan Didion, Vintage, 2007)

"Didion's husband, the writer John Gregory Dunne, died of a heart attack, just after they had returned from the hospital where their only child, Quintana, was lying in a coma. This book is a memoir of Dunne's death, Quintana's illness, and Didion's efforts to make sense of a time when nothing made sense." From *The New Yorker*

In the Slender Margin: An unflinching embrace of death's reality and persistent mystery (Eve Joseph, HarperCollins, 2014)

"In the Slender Margin is intended as an exploration rather than a balm or solace, though it will no doubt be those things for some people. Its resonance comes, rather, from its intelligent open-endedness, its unflinching, simultaneous embrace of death's reality and persistent mystery." From *The Globe and Mail*

Mortally Wounded: Stories of Soul Pain, Death, and Healing (Michael Kearney, Spring Journal Inc., 2007)

"Through somber stories, a hospice physician shares his experiences of working with people near death, revealing how the dying process can be a time of personal growth. Kearney, medical director of palliative care at Our Lady's Hospice in Dublin, Ireland, argues that the terror of death stems from a split between the rational and intuitive minds. When an individual becomes alienated from his deepest and most fundamental aspect, he says, the result is soul pain." From *Kirkus Reviews*

What Dying People Want: Practical Wisdom for the End Of Life (David Kuhl, PublicAffairs, 2003)

"Drawing from case studies that he conducted as part of the Soros Foundation's "Death in America" project, Kuhl provides a balanced perspective on caring for the terminally ill. An M.D. himself, he acknowledges that doctors sometimes have poor interpersonal skills, and he offers helpful insight into why this is so and how patients can foster better communication. Besides discussing the physician's account of the clinical aspects of the dying process, Kuhl sensitively examines the harder-to-define psychological and spiritual issues." From *Library Journal*

A Year to Live: How to Live This Year as If It Were Your Last (Stephen Levine. Three Rivers Press, 1998)
"As a counselor for the terminally ill and author of many works on spirituality and dying, Levine has come to believe that preparing for or "practicing" death reminds one of the beauty of life. In this production of his book (Crown, 1997), Levine himself relates his experiences and emotions in his yearlong experiment in "conscious living." From *Library Journal*

Facing Death and Finding Hope: A Guide to the Emotional and Spiritual Care Of The Dying (Christine Longaker. Main Street Books, 1998)
"Christine Longaker's experience with death and care of the dying began in 1976 when her husband was diagnosed with acute leukemia at the age of 24. Since his death, she has devoted her life to ease the suffering of those facing death. In a clear and compassionate tone, she identifies the typical fears and struggles experienced by the dying and their families. The core of the book is presented in "Four Tasks of Living and Dying," using the Tibetan Buddhist perspective on death to provide a new framework of meaning that can be applied to every type of caregiving setting. These spiritual principles are universal, enabling readers to find resonance within their own religious traditions." From the publisher

Dying: A Book of Comfort (Pat McNees. Grand Central Publishing, 1998)
"This remarkable collection, coming from personal experience and wide reading, will help many find the potential of growth through loss." Review by Dame Cicely Saunders, founder of the hospice movement

How We Die: Reflections of Life's Final Chapter (Sherwin B. Nuland, Vintage, 1995)

"Drawing upon his own broad experience and the characteristics of the six most common death-causing diseases, Nuland examines what death means to the doctor, patient, nurse, administrator, and family. Thought provoking and humane, his is not the usual syrup-and-generality approach to this well-worn topic." From *Booklist*

The Good Death: The New American Search to Reshape the End of Life (Marilyn Webb. Bantam, 1999)

"Webb's message is clear: The modern way of dying involves excessive emphasis on exotic technology and too little reliance on palliative care. The book is richly textured with personal, international, and cross-cultural suggestions for remedying the imbalance." From *Library Journal*

Grace and Grit: Spirituality and Healing in the Life and Death of Treya Killam Wilber (Ken Wilber, Shambhala, 2001)

"A tremendously moving love story. Wilber presents cancer as a healing crisis, an occasion for self-confrontation and growth." From *Publishers Weekly*

76 How to Establish a Life Stories Hospice Program

Those of you interested in building a sustainable life stories program at your local hospice will need more than good will and enthusiasm—

although that helps. I hope that the experience I gained in establishing a life stories service at Victoria Hospice will be of help to you.

One of the factors that weighed in my favor was the growing academic research supporting the value of life stories. It's not uncommon for some medical professionals to see life stories as a frill, not something that can complement end-of-life support. Being armed with the relevant research can bolster your proposal.

Here's a suggestion. Before attempting to initiate a hospice life stories program, familiarize yourself with the research. Two studies in particular that I'd recommend are:

- *Dignity Therapy: A Novel Psychotherapeutic Intervention for Patients Near the End of Life.* Harvey Max Chochinov, Thomas Hack, Thomas Hassard, Linda J. Kristjanson, Susan McClement, and Mike Harlos. *Journal of Clinical Oncology.* 2005; Vol. 23, No. 24

  Ninety-one percent of participants reported being satisfied with Dignity Therapy; 76% reported a heightened sense of dignity; 68% an increased sense of purpose; 67% a heightened sense of meaning; 47% an increased will to live; 81% reported that it had already, or would be of help to their family.

- *Legacy Activities as Interventions Approaching the End of Life.* Rebecca S. Allen, Michelle M. Hilgeman, Margaret A. Ege, John L. Shuster, Louis D. Burgio. *Journal of Palliative Medicine.* September 2008, 11(7): 1029-1038.

Intervention patients reported decreased breathing difficulty and increased religious meaning. Caregivers and patients reported greater social interaction on the part of the patient. All participants in the intervention group initiated a Legacy activity and reported that Legacy improved family communication. Legacy interventions hold promise and are simple to implement.

Other studies of older people and reminiscence have also shown promising results. One in particular is:

- *Evaluating the Impact of Reminiscence on the Quality of Life of Older People.* A report by the Economic and Social Research Council about a piece of research on reminiscence they carried out with 142 older people in 2003.

   Reminiscence activity results in psychological benefit for older people. Older people in our study who participated in activities were found at the end of the period of intervention to have better psychological morale and less psychological morbidity, and show more positive emotion and less negative emotion, than older people in our study who had not participated in our activities.

A pioneer in the interdisciplinary study of aging is Robert N. Butler. One of his seminal articles, "Age, Death, and Life Review," is a must read. This article originally appeared in *Living With Grief: Loss in Later Life*, Kenneth J. Doka, Editor, © Hospice Foundation of America, 2002.

The life review, as sometimes manifested by nostalgia and reminiscence, is a natural healing process. It represents one of the underlying human capacities on which all psychotherapy depends. Some of the positive results of a life review can be the righting of old wrongs, making up with estranged family members or friends, coming to accept one's mortality, and gaining a sense of serenity, pride in accomplishment, and a feeling of having done one's best.

I want to highlight five other factors to consider when establishing a life stories program at your local hospice. If you want to be credible and succeed, here's what to do:

1. *Become a hospice volunteer.* This is the route I took. If you're going to work with people at the end of life, it helps immeasurably if you're trained as a hospice volunteer. First, you gain experience and a level of comfort being with people who are dying. Second, it signals to the hospice administration that you are serious and committed to helping patients in palliative care. Third, and most importantly, you become a familiar and trusted part of the hospice care team.

2. *Keep your hospice "life stories" work separate from your personal history business.* It's critical to your success in establishing a program to assure hospice administration that you're not using the hospice to recruit clients for your business. I've been scrupulous in not mixing my business with my hospice work.

3. *Find a hospice manager who'll champion your idea.* In most cases this individual will be the person responsible for volunteer

services or it might be the manager of psychosocial services or spiritual care. This will be the person you'll need to convince that a life stories program is worthwhile and complements other hospice services. This manager will also have to bring other members of the hospice management team on board with your idea. It's important that you establish a good rapport with your "champion."

4. *Keep it simple.* You want to keep the time and costs involved to a minimum, especially because you're providing a free service. This is why the program I initiated at Victoria Hospice only offers unedited audio recordings of patient interviews. Do make sure that the hospice covers the cost of any materials you provide.

5. *Build in a program to train other life story volunteers.* It's inevitable that you'll soon find there are more requests than you can handle. Besides, you'll not be able to devote all your time to offering a free service unless you're fabulously wealthy! Here's another point to take into consideration: ideally, you should be planning for a program that will continue even when you're no longer involved.

77 Life Stories and Palliative Care: Your Questions Answered

One of my presentations at a previous Association of Personal Historians conference was *Life Stories as Healing: Working in an End-of-Life Environment.* In the workshop we looked at some of the skills needed and challenges faced in providing life stories for patients receiving palliative care.

Near the end of our session I asked participants to write down one "burning question" they wanted answered. We had time for only a few. I decided that for those who didn't have their questions answered I would deal with them here. I thought that those of you who weren't at my workshop might also appreciate seeing the questions and answers.

How does one set up a personal history program with a hospice?

There is no one right way to set up a program. Much will depend on the local circumstances. From my experience with Victoria Hospice I've learned a few lessons and passed these along in How to Establish a Life Stories Hospice Program (76).

Why not charge for life stories work at a hospice? Why should this work be voluntary?

If you're a professional personal historian, you can request a fee from your hospice for your services or provide it pro bono. That decision is really up to you and your hospice. As a rule, I don't volunteer my professional services. What I do at Victoria Hospice is volunteer on a regular shift just like the other volunteers. I've been doing that for ten years.

With regards to the Life Stories program I established, I trained 12 hospice volunteers, nine of whom are actively engaged in the work. I designed and ran the training programs and for that I was paid my regular fee. I don't do life story interviews with patients unless there is no one else available.

I still continue to do some of the co-ordination and management of the program on a voluntary basis but I'm working to hand this over eventually to other volunteers. My goal is to have the Life Stories program be totally self-sufficient without my involvement. From the beginning I made it clear to the Victoria Hospice administration that I wanted to see such a service succeed but that I did not want to continue to be involved in its day-to-day operation.

Are your hospice Life Stories volunteers paid and do the families pay for the service?

Our Life Stories volunteers, save one, are not professional personal historians and are not paid. They do this work as part of their contribution to Victoria Hospice. We do not charge families for this service.

I should add that from the beginning we decided to keep the service as simple and as cost effective as possible. We only provide unedited audio interviews transferred to CDs or USB drives.

How long is a typical Life Stories interview session?

To be honest there isn't really a typical session. So much depends on the condition of the patient. We don't schedule more than an hour but sessions can be as short as 10 or 15 minutes if the patient is weak or drowsy.

What is the typical time it takes for your volunteers to complete a personal history project?

Again, there is no typical length of time. We tell patients that they can use up to 5 hours of interview time to tell their story. Some manage that and others become too ill to continue beyond an hour or two. So much depends on the overall health of a patient when they start the process.

Given the fact that our patients are frail, it can sometimes take 6 or more weeks to complete 5 hours of interview.

What if the patient is resistant to talking at all?

Our Life Stories program is only offered to those Victoria Hospice patients who request it. At any time a patient may opt out of the Life Stories program if they find it not to their liking.

What event or events in your life made you decide to do this work?

I find it's often difficult to determine at what point an idea begins to germinate. I know that when I was 32, a dear friend died in a car crash. I had seen her just the day before. She was a vibrant and compassionate individual and then she was gone. From that moment I knew that "death" was a companion on my journey.

However, it wasn't until two decades later as a documentary filmmaker that I shot, directed, and edited a series for the National Film Board of Canada, entitled *Bearing Witness.* It followed three individuals who were living with a terminal illness.

As part of my research for that series I spent time at Victoria Hospice talking to nurses, counselors, doctors, and volunteers. I admired and I liked these people. I decided that once I had completed the series, I wanted to become a Victoria Hospice volunteer. In 2005 I completed my training and I've been working there ever since.

If you have only weeks to capture the essence of a patient's life, do you invite the family to finish telling the story?

So far, most of the patients who agree to our Life Stories interviews have only weeks to live. If we have six or seven weeks, we can usually record up to five hours of a person's life story. If it looks as if time is running out, we may skip to topics that the patient feels are crucial.

The Life Stories interviewer always works with a patient to determine what that patient wishes to record. In some cases it's a personal history from birth to the present. For others it might be a legacy letter or ethical will. It varies.

We haven't invited family members to complete a life story. They are usually too emotionally exhausted to consider such a request.

What do you do if you as the interviewer begin to cry?

As an interviewer I'm a human being with feelings. The stories I hear have moments that are sad and I feel sad. I try to keep in mind that this is my subject's story. It is not about me. I don't want to start crying and have the attention shift from my subject to me. There are times when what I hear makes my eyes moisten and I express my sorrow at my subject's plight. But I keep some reserve in that moment. I save the tears for later when I'm home and can receive the support I need from my partner.

Should one raise or not raise the issue of death?

I wish I could say that there's one rule fits all but so much depends on your subject and the rapport you've established. Some patients want to talk about facing death and others don't. What is important is to judge how comfortable you yourself are with death and talking about it.

I have asked some of my palliative care clients what they fear about death and in most cases they are quite open and honest with their reply. We need not shy away from talking about death but we must be sensitive to the needs of our clients.

Are men reluctant to discuss emotional issues? If they are, should the interviewer draw them out or respect their reluctance?

Male aversion to emotional issues is something of a generality and quite often true from my experience. Men prefer to talk about what they've done and where they've been than get into "messy" emotional stuff—not all men but a good number. In fairness though, to be facing your imminent death is tough and raises all kinds of feelings—anger, fear, grief, and panic. I've had some men and women who've made it clear to me that the only way they can get through the interviews is by avoiding highly charged subject matter. I respect their wishes.

When shown respect and compassion, it is not uncommon for men to go from a reluctance to talking about emotional matters to being quite open about their feelings. A word of caution. As personal historians we are not therapists. It's not our role to make people feel better. That's for the professional counselor. In fact we all need the names of several counselors we can refer our clients to, should the need arise.

Has pain on the part of a patient in palliative care interfered with your ability to help a person to tell their story?

For the most part pain is usually managed reasonably well by the time we start to work with a patient. However, there are other issues that can make it hard to record a person's story. People can become drowsy or at times muddled from the effects of their disease and medication. There can be bouts of nausea. Overwhelming fatigue can render people speechless. In these circumstances we wait until the patient has recovered sufficiently to continue. Sadly, in some cases, there is no recovery and the patient's story remains incomplete.

78 When Small Can Be Profound

Not long ago I was asked to audio record some final words from a young mother who was dying from cancer. I'll call her Sonia to protect the family's privacy. She was in her early 30s and she wanted to leave something for her only child, a five-year-old boy.

The day I met her, I asked what she would like to say to her little boy. It was not easy. The anguish of her never seeing her son again made it hard for Sonia to say what was in her heart. But with patience and time we were able to record a few minutes of her tender wishes and hopes for her boy.

I realized that we were not likely to get more. But a thought struck me. "What about bedtime stories?" I asked Sonia if she read to her boy and if he had some favorite stories. She smiled and nodded. "How would you like to select a couple and we could record you reading them?" She agreed, and on my next visit, although she was weak, she softly read the stories that her son had enjoyed. That was the last thing we recorded. Not long after Sonia died.

In all we had recorded little more than half an hour. Not much really. But as I thought about her son and the wonderful gift his mother had left, I was deeply moved. It wasn't a question of the amount we had recorded. It was that Sonia's little boy would still be able to hear her comforting voice. And one day, as a man, he would be able to listen to those bedside stories and remember his mother, a mother who died much too soon. Small can indeed be profound.

CHAPTER 12

For Do-It-Yourself Clients

Author's Note: Some of the articles in this chapter were written for my blog before I began to focus on the personal historian. They deserve a place in this book since the articles could be used by personal historians as support for clients who don't want full services but need some guidance. The articles could also be handouts at workshops or speaking engagements.

79 Do You Practice What You Preach?

As personal historians we don't always practice what we preach.

I'm sometimes asked if I've ever had my life story told. I haven't. And I always feel awkward about my response. I usually mutter that I'm too busy doing other people's stories. It's not a very satisfactory answer.

If I don't see the value of preserving my history, why should anyone believe me when I tell them the great advantages of preserving their own?

Now the fact is that I'm an only child and I don't have any children of my own. There aren't any family members to leave my life story to. A few of my friends might be interested but that's about it. So part of me thinks, "Why bother?"

I once made a request of my colleagues at the Association of Personal Historians. I asked, "What could you say that would inspire me to do my life story?" Their responses boil down to these five:

1. *It's an opportunity for reflection, insights, and renewal.*
2. *Friends and colleagues want to know the person behind the blog.*
3. *My life's been interesting and it should be documented.*
4. *My personal view of the events that have shaped my past are part of our collective oral history.*
5. *I'll be more empathetic of my clients as they work through their life stories.*

As great as these are, it was an e-mail response from Bruce Summers, a fellow member of the Association of Personal Historians, that moved me the most. I was reminded again of the power of storytelling. And how stories can be far more effective than facts and arguments in touching our hearts. I asked Bruce for permission to reprint his story. He kindly agreed.

Do yourself a favor and read this lovely reminiscence and its convincing argument for the need to record our life stories.

Joe & Helen
by Bruce Summers

Growing up I lived next to Joe and Helen Sitler. They were an older couple with no children. Joe had no brothers and sisters and he was the end of the Sitler line. We loved Helen. She was like a third grandmother to us. Joe was a bit gruff. He would not let us play in his yard, especially when he was mowing. He was afraid that the lawn tractor might throw a stone and hit me or one of my three brothers. In middle school I shared a bit of Joe's story in an article I wrote for the school magazine. People thought I made it up, notably the parts about what I had learned from Joe.

Later when Joe was very ill and nearing death, my older brother and I went over and helped Helen move him. He was skin and bones. Helen needed help so she could give him a sponge bath and change his linens. Joe died soon after. This was my first encounter with the death of a friend and a neighbor. Even though he was a bit gruff, he was Helen's husband and because of this he was a special man. They used to love to go to the city and dance to the music of the big bands when they came to town. He was born in the 19th century and had lived a full life and retired before I knew him. Most importantly he captured Helen's heart and had been a good husband. I missed Joe and 40 years later still treasure my memories of him.

Another eight or so years later after I graduated from college, I had the privilege of house-sitting in Joe and Helen Sitler's house. This was after she herself had grown older, more feeble and hard of hearing and needed to be in a nursing home. Her hearing aids did not really work well and it was hard to talk with her, hard to share with her how important she and Joe had been as our older grandparent-like neighbors, too late to tell her that I felt a little bad for stealing some of the grapes each year that Joe grew on his grape arbor just five feet from the border of our yard. I wished too late that I knew more about Joe and Helen who had no descendants and no relatives that we knew. They were our neighbors. They were our friends and they shared part of our lives growing up.

As I sat in their living room and slept in a bed in one of their bedrooms, cooked my meals at their table, wrote newspaper stories on my typewriter at their dining table, as I explored their home, the time capsule that they had lived in, I wondered about their lives. I remembered that Joe never let Helen turn on the electric lights. They used candles and were very frugal. She canned vegetables and fruits. The jars were in the basement in the back room on a built-in shelf made just for that purpose.

I finally left that house to join the Peace Corps. I visited Helen to say goodbye, realizing that I would likely never see her again. When she died, I asked my parents to purchase an old high-backed walnut chair from their living room. It was the one I sat in to watch TV or to write letters to my future wife late at night. I wanted to have a piece of their story since I was never going to have any written history.

I am left with memories of Helen and Joe—my good and my gruff neighbors. They have no descendants. They are the last of their line but are not yet forgotten forty years after they both had died.

Perhaps you will or will not decide to write your story—a bit of a legacy to the rest of us and to friends and colleagues, many of us very virtual and little known to you. I enjoy your blog posts. I very much enjoy the stories you tell and I admire your work and your background. You never know for sure who will read, who will remember, who will retell or share your story. It might mean a great deal to many of us to know a bit more about the man behind the camera and the man behind the blog. Good luck with your decision.

80 5 Surefire Ways to Kick-Start the Writing of Your Life Story

Probably the hardest part of writing your life story is actually getting started. There are all kinds of excuses. Do any of these sound familiar? I'm too busy. I'm too tired. I don't know what to say. The creative muse hasn't struck me. Well, here are five surefire ways you can use to kick-start your writing.

1. Keep a date with yourself.

Set aside a 30-minute block of time when you won't be disturbed. Mark it down in your calendar. Now here's the important part. For 30 minutes begin writing about some aspect of your life. It doesn't matter what. Just write. Don't stop. Don't worry about grammar or composition—just write. At the end of 30 minutes, stop. Get up from your desk and walk away. Congratulations! You've started your life story and you can come back and edit what you've written on another day.

2. Select a topic.

It helps if you can focus your attention on a particular topic that holds some interest for you. Here are a few suggestions to get you started.

- My idea of happiness.
- The individual who had the greatest influence on my life.
- The qualities I admire in a friend.
- A childhood memory.

3. Choose a favorite object.

We all have some favorite object that has been a part of our lives for some time. Mine is a little Nigerian thorn carving I collected many years ago when I was a volunteer in West Africa. Select your favorite object and write a story about how it came into your possession and what it means to you.

4. Pick a photograph.

Look through your photo collection until you find a picture that brings back a lot of memories. Now write about that photo. Where was it taken? Who's in it? What was happening?

5. Use a voice recorder.

If you're finding it hard to write out your story, why not try dictating it? Start by putting down five or six questions that you're going to ask yourself. Next, turn on the recorder and interview yourself. Later transcribe your interview and edit it.

Good luck! I'm sure that at least one of these ideas will get you started on your life story.

81 How to Get Started on Your Life Story

In life stories workshops, one of the questions people frequently ask me is, "How do I get started?" I thought that was an excellent question to address here. This is what I'd suggest.

Start by reading some reference books.

There are many excellent self-help books on writing your life story. Here are five that I'd recommend.

1. *How to Write Your Own Life Story: The Classic Guide for the Nonprofessional Writer* by Lois Daniel

2. *Legacy: A Step-By-Step Guide to Writing Personal History* by Linda Spence

3. *Writing Your Life: An Easy-to-Follow Guide to Writing an Autobiography* by Mary Borg

4. *Shimmering Images: A Handy Little Guide to Writing Memoir* by Lisa Dale Norton

5. *Writing Life Stories* by Bill Roorbach

Choose a format that appeals to you.

There are many different ways to record your story. Here are three.

1. *Chronological.* Organize your writing by following the stages of your life from birth and childhood through to adolescence and adulthood.

2. *Turning points.* Write about those moments when your life took a turn such as the death of a parent, the birth of your first child, a life threatening illness, loss of a job, or retirement.

3. *Thematic.* You could write vignettes around themes such as the values you've lived by, life lessons learned, the most memorable person you've known, or your accomplishments.

Make a date with yourself.

After you've selected an approach, decide what time of the day, what days of the week, and how long you can devote to writing. Mark those days and times in your calendar and stick to them.

Start writing.

The trick here is just to write and keep writing until your time is up. Write the way you talk. Don't worry about being perfect. Editing and polishing can come later.

None of the above.

You might want to try one of the many online life story programs like "Personal Historian 2" or "Story of My Life."

82 6 Reasons Why Writing Your Life Story Matters

Maybe you're like a number of people who say, "Yeah, I've thought about writing my life story, but…(fill in the blank)." There are all kinds of excuses for not getting down to it. That's why I've put together this list to get you motivated.

I'm convinced that after reading these six reasons for writing your life story you'll want to get started today…or maybe tomorrow. But you will start. Right?

1. You're the only one who really knows your story.

How will you be remembered? Will friends and relatives be the ones to define you after you're gone? I don't know about you, but I'd rather be the one to describe who I am and what motivates me.

2. Your life story is a gift.

This is no time to be modest and humble. While you may think your life has been of no great significance, others will beg to differ. I now have my mother's story told in a beautiful 117-page hardcover book. I will treasure this book for as long as I live, because it is a very tangible reminder of who she is. It is a gift.

3. Your story is part of a country's oral history.

Writing about the life you have lived is a window on another time and place. It can provide a rich and personal glimpse into daily life and major events of the day. Generations to come will find it fascinating and educational to know how you lived.

4. Recording your life story can be therapeutic.

Academic studies show that the act of reviewing one's life can bring a sense of accomplishment and peace of mind. By reflecting on our life we begin to see that it is not a series of random events but that there is a discernible pattern. It helps us make sense of our lives and explains why we did the things we did. Looking back on my life, I realize that the many different things I've done have all been connected with my need to be of service.

5. Your life story can be of help to others.

Our lives are filled with challenges. How we cope with them and the lessons we've learned can be of benefit to others.

6. A life story connects the generations.

In today's world families are more often than not scattered across vast distances. We no longer share stories around the supper table. Young people don't know their roots. A life story provides one way to reconnect families and bring them the richness of their heritage.

83 A Proven System That Will Get Your Life Story Completed

If you've wanted to get your life story written, then why not do it now? Here's one of the best approaches I've found for tackling big projects. I learned it from David Allen's fantastic book, *Getting Things Done.* If you haven't read it, I strongly urge you to pick up a copy. He rightly points out that when we are faced with something huge to do, we become overwhelmed and either avoid work on it or start and stop in an erratic and demoralized fashion.

For most of us, writing our life story can seem a daunting task. Where to begin? What Allen suggests is that you break down a project into small manageable tasks called actions. You know—it's like the old joke, "How do you eat an elephant? One bite at a time!" Yuk! Yuk!

But seriously folks…here's what I'd suggest. Begin by making a list of tasks you need to do to get your book launched. Start with the first thing you need to do, followed by the next logical step or action. For example, a possible list of your Next Actions could look like this:

1. Research and find several book titles about writing a life story.

2. Go to the local library or bookstore.

3. Select at least two books on writing a life story.

4. Read two chapters of Book One every day until completed.

5. Read Book Two committing to two chapters a day until completed.

6. Purchase a 7-by-10 lined notebook in which to write draft.

7. Determine a time and place to do writing.

8. Begin writing by answering the following, "What are my earliest childhood memories?"

I'm not saying that this is what your list should look like. You may have a quite different set of actions and that's just fine. The important point is to keep each of your steps simple and in a logical order. If you find that one of your Next Actions contains several steps, then break it down again until you have a series of simple manageable actions.

Warning: don't try to organize your whole book-writing project from beginning to end in one sitting. You'll be overwhelmed. I'd recommend that you stop your planning when you get to the point where you're uncertain what Next Action you should take. Once you work through your Next Actions list it will become clearer what you need to do next.

84 Do You Make These Mistakes When Writing Your Life Story?

I've helped people edit their life story and found that these are some of the most common mistakes.

Writing in a voice that's not your own.

Write the way you talk. Your life story is for your family—not for the general public. If you think that you have to sound "learned" or "writerly" then you'll only succeed in sounding phony. People want to hear your story in your voice.

Writing long convoluted sentences.

Simple is better. Look at your sentence and see if it wouldn't be better broken down into two or even three sentences. Remember Hemingway.

Beginning almost every sentence with "I."

Hey, it's your story and I know it's hard not to keep saying "I." Take a hard look at one of your paragraphs and see where you can cut some of the "I"s.

Repeating the same word or phrase over and over and over again.

Sometimes it works…like my preceding sentence. On the whole though "writing ticks" can be really distracting to the reader. Go over your work and see where you can drop some of your repetitions.

Failing to think of a beginning, middle and end for your paragraph or chapter.

A quick way to lose your reader is to fail to give them a sense of where you're going. You might want to tease your reader with the ending and then build their curiosity as to how that ending came to be. Or you can start more conventionally at the beginning and work to a conclusion. It doesn't really matter as long as you're clear about the path you're taking.

Mixing several different topics, ideas or themes into the same paragraph.

Don't create a jumble of thoughts. It's like getting lost in a giant crowded shopping mall without any clear exit. It creates confusion, stress, and claustrophobia. Check to see where you could drop some passages and put them in another section of your story.

85 8 Tips on Writing Your Life Story

1. Write the way you talk.

It's your story and it should sound like you. Forget about style. Worrying about style is one of the surest ways to develop writer's block.

2. Your story is more than places and events.

Make sure you share your insights, feelings and beliefs about the people and events that you've encountered. This will give your life story depth and warmth.

3. Remember the details.

It is the details that enrich your story. While they may seem uninteresting to you, they will most certainly be of interest to your descendants.

4. Start your story wherever you want.

You don't have to begin with your birth and then work through the years chronologically. You could begin with a key event or the most significant person in your life.

5. Don't forget the tears and laughter.

Our lives are not all sweetness and light. Leaving out the struggles, conflicts, disappointments, pratfalls, and humor will create a life story with little reality or interest. Be as candid as you can without hurting or embarrassing someone.

6. Make a date with yourself.

When are you the most relaxed and reflective? In the early morning, during a mid-afternoon tea break or late in the evening before bed? Pick a time that works best for you, mark it in your calendar, and make a practice of using this time on a regular basis to work on your writing.

7. Put your Gremlins on hold.

Our inner critics love to sabotage any new venture. So beware of the Gremlins telling you that, "No one's interested in your story." "Who said you could write?" "This is boring." Tell your Gremlins to get lost. And continue writing.

8. Bring historical events into your life story.

References to historical events will provide your readers with a better sense of the time and place of your story.

86 How to Write a Life Story People Will Really Want to Read

If you want people to enjoy reading your life story then consider these six tips to better writing. I guarantee it'll put a little "zest" into your prose.

1. Keep your audience in mind.

Don't think you have to write a best seller. Your book is for family and friends. They're the ones who will really enjoy reading about your life. If you think you're writing to be published you'll get all "cramped up" and your natural style will suffer.

2. Be authentic.

Write the way you talk. This follows from what I said above. People want to hear your authentic "voice" coming through in the writing. That's what makes it real to them. If you try to emulate the style of a best-selling author you're likely to produce something affected, unintentionally funny, and ultimately unreadable.

3. Touch people's hearts.

Make certain that you tell your readers what you were feeling—not just what you were doing. For example, "The night I caught the train East I

193

felt a mixture of excitement and sadness. I was leaving home—a young man of 22, bound for two years in Africa as a volunteer. As the train pulled out of the station, I can still see my mother's face awash in tears." This has more emotional impact than writing, "I caught the train east, heading for a two year assignment as a volunteer in Africa."

4. Use all of your senses.

When you're describing a particular event or scene, bring your sense of taste, touch, smell, sight, and hearing to enrich your writing. For example, "Every Monday my mother baked bread. Even today, the aroma of freshly baked bread brings back vivid memories. I'd hover round those golden brown loaves, just out of the oven, waiting for my mom's permission to cut myself a piece. When they had cooled, I'd hack through a still warm loaf—slather a slice with butter and chomp down. It was pure heaven!" This is far more interesting than writing, "My mother baked bread once a week. It was one of my favorite treats."

5. Keep your focus.

Make sure you don't ramble off topic. It's a sure way to slow down your story. Let's say you're writing about your first job. Don't halfway through start describing a vacation you took with a friend—unless there is some direct link to your work.

6. Vary your sentence length.

Take a look at one of your paragraphs. Are all your sentences about the same length? This makes for tedious reading. Aim to have a variety of sentences—short, long and medium. As they say, variety is the spice of life!

87 Are You Letting Treasured Memories Slip Away?

Memories are like summer clouds—ephemeral and soon gone. Here are five ways you can start now to preserve your special memories.

1. Begin to scan and identify all of your family photos.

Write a note with each photo indicating the place, date, event and who is in the picture.

2. Use a digital voice recorder and begin describing your childhood.

Include things such as favorite memories, places you lived, pets you loved and celebrations.

3. Create a list of 30 things about yourself.

Think of it as a mini autobiography. If future generations were to know 30 things about you what would they be?

4. Keep a "Memory Jar."

Plan once a day to write down one favorite memory from anytime in your life and add it to the jar. After a month, take out your memories, print them on good quality paper and give them to your family.

5. Keep a "Gratitude Journal."

At the end of each day take time to reflect on what you are grateful for that day.

88 4 Unique Ways to Tell a Life Story

A life story doesn't have to be produced as a book, DVD, or CD. Here are some other ideas to get you thinking out of the box.

1. A Six-Word Memoir.

Smith Magazine has been collecting six-word memoirs from readers and compiling them into books. Check them out at www.sixwordmemoirs.com. One of my favorites is "I still make coffee for two" by Zak Nelson. Larry Smith, the creative brains behind Smith Magazine says: "There's no longer any debate: you can absolutely tell a compelling, poignant, and/or funny story in just six words. But six words aren't necessarily the end—they can be a beginning. We've heard from many writers whose six-word memoir spurred them on to write thousands more." What is your Six-Word Memoir?

2. A Life Story Quilt.

A dying mother of two teenage girls first introduced me to this idea. She had survived cancer for some 8 years. Over that time she gathered all kinds of "stuff" connected with her children's growing up. On her last Christmas she transformed this material into two beautiful quilts for her daughters. Here are two other examples of life story quilts: The Journey to the White House Quilt (http://www.joangaither.com/) and The Quilted Conscience (http://www.gicf.org/news-and-events/latest-news/The-Quilted-Conscience).

3. A Life Story Box.

Find an attractive "archival quality" box large enough to hold a lifetime of memories. Into your time capsule place your photo albums, home movies, old letters, favorite recipes, airline boarding passes, theater and concert tickets, high school and university year books, certificates, old passports, etc. I would take the time to carefully number each of the items and include a list that identifies the significance of each. This is particularly important for future generations who will need some help to identify, for example, the importance of an old concert ticket you've included in the box.

4. A Graphic Life Story.

If you have an artistic flair, why not think of your life story or that of a loved one in terms of hand illustrated panels. Can't draw? Then consider hiring an illustrator. Too expensive? Try checking out a college or university fine arts program. It might be possible to find a student willing to work with you as part of her studies.

89 How to Write Your Life Story in 20 Statements

Still putting off writing your life story?

Well here's something you might want to try. Write down a list of twenty statements about yourself that would give someone in the future an idea of who you are. Skip the physical descriptions. It takes some reflection but it's quicker than writing a book and it's fun. To give you an idea of what I'm talking about, I'll put down a few things about me—not everything, of course!

- I am a practicing Buddhist.
- I love cats.
- I value loyalty, integrity, and humor.
- I'm an only child.
- I like to dance.
- I enjoy solitude.
- My favorite colors are blue and green.
- I'm punctual and don't appreciate people who are tardy.
- I'm patient and persistent.
- I believe, as Gandhi said, we have to be the change we want to see in the world.

Now it's your turn. One of the things you can do after completing your list is use your statements as jumping off points for writing your book. For example, each of my statements above could be expanded into a chapter. It's a different way of structuring your life story but it works!

CHAPTER 13:
Inspiration for Personal Historians

90 15 Great Memoirs Written by Men

I dislike modern memoirs. They are generally written by people who have either entirely lost their memories, or have never done anything worth remembering. ~ Oscar Wilde

Oscar Wilde's wit could well apply to many of today's memoirs. But the truth is that among the deluge of memoirs published every year there are some gems. Here it is—a totally subjective listing but all terrific reads. Credit for the summaries goes to the listed sources.

Experience: A Memoir by Martin Amis
The son of the great comic novelist Kingsley Amis, Martin Amis explores his relationship with this father and writes about the various crises of Kingsley's life. He also examines the life and legacy of his

cousin, Lucy Partington, who was abducted and murdered by one of Britain's most notorious serial killers. Experience also deconstructs the changing literary scene, including Amis' portraits of Saul Bellow, Salman Rushdie, Allan Bloom, Philip Larkin, and Robert Graves, among others. ~ from *Amazon.com*

Goodbye to All That by Robert Graves
In 1929 Robert Graves went to live abroad permanently, vowing "never to make England my home again." This is his superb account of his life up until that 'bitter leave-taking' from his childhood and desperately unhappy school days at Charterhouse, to his time serving as a young officer in the First World War that was to haunt him throughout his life. ~ from *Amazon.com*

Dispatches by Michael Herr
American correspondent Herr's documentary recalls the heavy combat he witnessed in Vietnam as well as the obscene speech, private fears, and nightmares of the soldiers. "Herr captures the almost hallucinatory madness of the war," said *Publishers Weekly*. "This is a compelling, truth-telling book with a visceral impact, its images stuck in the mind like shards from a pineapple bomb." ~ from *Publishers Weekly*

All Creatures Great and Small by James Herriot
In *All Creatures Great and Small,* we meet the young Herriot as he takes up his calling and discovers that the realities of veterinary practice in rural Yorkshire are very different from the sterile setting of veterinary school. From caring for his patients in the depths of winter on the remotest homesteads to dealing with uncooperative owners and critically ill animals, Herriot discovers the wondrous variety and never-ending

challenges of veterinary practice as his humor, compassion, and love of the animal world shine forth. ~ from *Amazon.com*

Wordstruck: A Memoir by Robert MacNeil
People become writers, in large part, because they are in love with language. *Wordstruck* is the story of one such writer's unabashed affair with words, from his Halifax childhood awash with intriguing incidents to life as a traveling journalist who "delighted in finding pockets of distinctive English, as a botanist is thrilled to discover a new variety of plant." ~ from *goodreads.com*

Angela's Ashes by Frank McCourt
"Worse than the ordinary miserable childhood is the miserable Irish childhood," writes Frank McCourt in *Angela's Ashes*. "Worse yet is the miserable Irish Catholic childhood." Welcome, then, to the pinnacle of the miserable Irish Catholic childhood. Born in Brooklyn in 1930 to recent Irish immigrants Malachy and Angela McCourt, Frank grew up in Limerick after his parents returned to Ireland because of poor prospects in America. ~ from *Amazon.com*

A Million Miles in a Thousand Years: What I Learned While Editing My Life by Donald Miller
Miller, the accidental memoirist who struck gold with the likable ramble Blue Like Jazz, writes about the challenges inherent in getting unstuck creatively and spiritually. After Jazz sold more than a million copies but his other books didn't follow suit, he had a classic case of writer's block. Two movie producers contacted him about creating a film out of his life, but Miller's initial enthusiasm was dampened when they concluded that

his real life needed doctoring lest it be too directionless for the screen. ~ from *Publishers Weekly*

Becoming a Man: Half a Life Story by Paul Monette
… poetic yet highly political, angry yet infused with the love of life—is what transforms *Becoming a Man* from simple autobiography into an intense record of struggle and salvation. Paul Monette did not lead a life different from many gay men—he struggled courageously with his family, his sexuality, his AIDS diagnosis—but in bearing witness to his and others' pain, he creates a personal testimony that illuminates the darkest corners of our culture even as it finds unexpected reserves of hope. ~ from *Amazon.com*

Speak, Memory by Vladimir Nabokov
[Nabokov] has fleshed the bare bones of historical data with hilarious anecdotes and with a felicity of style that makes *Speak, Memory* a constant pleasure to read. Confirmed Nabokovians will relish the further clues and references to his fictional works that shine like nuggets in the silver stream of his prose. ~ from *Harper's*

Steinbeck: A Life in Letters by John Steinbeck
Nobel Prize-winner John Steinbeck was a prolific correspondent. Opening with letters written during Steinbeck's early years in California, and closing with an unfinished 1968 note written in Sag Harbor, New York, this collection of around 850 letters to friends, family, his editor, and a diverse circle of well-known and influential public figures gives an insight into the raw creative processes of one of the most naturally-gifted and hard-working writing minds of this century. ~ from *Amazon.com*

Darkness Visible: A Memoir of Madness by William Styron
A meditation on Styron's (*Sophie's Choice*) serious depression at the age
of 60, this essay evokes with detachment and dignity the months-long
turmoil whose symptoms included the novelist's "dank joylessness,"
insomnia, physical aversion to alcohol (previously "an invaluable senior
partner of my intellect"), and his persistent "fantasies of self-
destruction" leading to psychiatric treatment and hospitalization. ~ from
Publishers Weekly

Self-Consciousness by John Updike
Updike's memoir—it is by no means an autobiography, but rather, as the
title brilliantly suggests, a thoughtful communing with past selves—is, as
expected, wonderfully written. It is also disarmingly frank about certain
aspects of the writer's life. Updike discusses his psoriasis and stuttering,
his parents and failures as husband and father, his politics, the ways in
which God permeates his life, and his profound commitment to writing.
~ from *Publishers Weekly*

Night by Elie Wiesel
In Nobel laureate Elie Wiesel's memoir *Night,* a scholarly, pious teenager
is wracked with guilt at having survived the horror of the Holocaust and
the genocidal campaign that consumed his family. His memories of the
nightmare world of the death camps present him with an intolerable
question: how can the God he once so fervently believed in have allowed
these monstrous events to occur? There are no easy answers in this
harrowing book, which probes life's essential riddles with the lucid
anguish only great literature achieves. It marks the crucial first step in

Wiesel's lifelong project to bear witness for those who died. ~ from *Amazon.com*

This Boy's Life: A Memoir by Tobias Wolff
In PEN/Faulkner Award-winner Wolff's fourth book, he recounts his coming-of-age with customary skill and self-assurance. Seeking a better life in the Northwestern U.S. with his divorced mother, whose "strange docility, almost paralysis, with men of the tyrant breed" taught Wolff the virtue of rebellion, he considered himself "in hiding," moved to invent a private, "better" version of himself in order to rise above his troubles. ~ from *Publishers Weekly*

Black Boy by Richard Wright
Autobiography by Richard Wright, published in 1945 and considered to be one of his finest works... From the 1960s the work came to be understood as the story of Wright's coming of age and development as a writer whose race, though a primary component of his life, was but one of many that formed him as an artist. ~ from *The Merriam-Webster Encyclopedia of Literature*

91 15 Great Memoirs Written by Women

I don't know about you but I find a friend's assessment of a book is often as good, if not better than, that of some of the reviewers. That's why I wanted to share with you this list, compiled by some of my colleagues in the Association of Personal Historians. Here are fifteen gems to add to your list of summer reading. Credit for the summaries goes to the listed sources.

An American Childhood by Annie Dillard
Dillard's luminous prose painlessly captures the pain of growing up in this wonderful evocation of childhood. Her memoir is partly a hymn to Pittsburgh, where orange streetcars ran on Penn Avenue in 1953 when she was eight, and where the Pirates were always in the cellar. ~ from *Publishers Weekly*

Pilgrim At Tinker Creek by Annie Dillard
The book is a form of meditation, written with headlong urgency, about seeing. A reader's heart must go out to a young writer with a sense of wonder so fearless and unbridled...There is an ambition about her book that I like...It is the ambition to feel. ~ Eudora Welty, *New York Times Book Review*

Balsamroot: A Memoir by Mary Clearman Blew
Blew mines the repository of her aunt's memoirs and diaries, uncovering near-revelations that suggest Imogene's life was far from what it appeared to be. The memoir is energized by the search and by the author's connectedness to a Montana heritage. ~ from *Publishers Weekly*

Bone Deep in Landscape: Writing, Reading, and Place by Mary Clearman Blew
"I cannot reconcile myself to the loss of landscape, which for me often is an analogy for my own body.... And yet I know that I have never owned the landscape." In her second collection of essays (after *All But the Waltz*), Blew again demonstrates her artistry and strong connection to

the Western terrain of her past and present homes in Montana and Idaho. ~ from *Publishers Weekly*

A Girl Named Zippy: Growing Up Small in Mooreland, Indiana by Haven Kimmel
It's a cliché, to say that a good memoir reads like a well-crafted work of fiction, but Kimmel's smooth, impeccably humorous prose evokes her childhood as vividly as any novel. ~ from *Publishers Weekly*

The Leopard Hat: A Daughter's Story by Valerie Steiker
In this finely etched memoir, Steiker relives her childhood in the family apartment on Manhattan's Upper West Side, the Parisian escapes with her mother, and the family holidays in India and Nepal in delicious, Proustian detail. ~ from *Publishers Weekly*

Little Heathens: Hard Times and High Spirits on an Iowa Farm During the Great Depression by Mildred Armstrong Kalish
Simple, detailed and honest, this is a refreshing and informative read for anyone interested in the struggles of average Americans in the thick of the Great Depression. ~ from *Publishers Weekly*

Lazy B by Sandra Day O'Connor
A collaboration between O'Connor and her brother, the book recounts the lives of their parents "MO" and "DA" (pronounced "M.O." and "D.A.") and the colorful characters who helped run the Lazy B ranch. ~ from *Publishers Weekly*

The Woman Warrior: Memoirs of a Girlhood Among Ghosts by Maxine Hong Kingston

The Woman Warrior is a pungent, bitter, but beautifully written memoir of growing up Chinese American in Stockton, California. ~ from *Amazon.com Review*

Personal History by Katharine Graham

This is the story of a newspaper's rise to power but also of the destruction of a marriage, as Philip Graham slid into alcohol, depression, and suicide, and of Katharine's rise as a powerful woman in her own right. ~ from *Library Journal*

Some Memories of a Long Life [1854-1911] by Malvina Shanklin Harlan

These memoirs by the wife of a noted Supreme Court justice, John Marshall Harlan, first appeared in the Journal of Supreme Court History.... Justice Harlan, though a former slave-holder, is remembered for his lone and eloquent dissent in Plessy v. Ferguson, the case that established the doctrine of "separate but equal." ~ from *Publishers Weekly*

The Road from Coorain by Jill Ker Conway

At age 11, Conway (Women Reformers and American Culture) left the arduous life on her family's sheep farm in the Australian outback for school in war-time Sydney, burdened by an emotionally dependent, recently widowed mother. A lively curiosity and penetrating intellect illuminate this unusually objective account of the author's progress from a solitary childhood—the most appealing part of the narrative—to public achievement as president of Smith College and now professor at MIT. ~ from *Publishers Weekly*

The Prize Winner of Defiance, Ohio: How My Mother Raised 10 Kids on 25 Words or Less by Terry Ryan

Married to a man with violent tendencies and a severe drinking problem, Evelyn Ryan managed to keep her 10 children fed and housed during the 1950s and '60s by entering—and winning—contests for rhymed jingles and advertising slogans of 25-words-or-less. This engaging and quick-witted biography written by daughter Terry... relates how Evelyn submitted multiple entries, under various names, for contests sponsored by Dial soap, Lipton soup, Paper Mate pens, Kleenex Tissues and any number of other manufacturers, and won a wild assortment of prizes, including toasters, bikes, basketballs, and all-you-can-grab supermarket shopping sprees. ~ from *Publishers Weekly*

Wait Till Next Year: A Memoir by Doris Kearns Goodwin

Goodwin recounts some wonderful stories in this coming-of-age tale about both her family and an era when baseball truly was the national pastime that brought whole communities together. From details of specific games to descriptions of players, including Jackie Robinson, a great deal of the narrative centers around the sport. ~ from *Library Journal*

A Romantic Education by Patricia Hampl

A now-classic memoir, described by Doris Grumbach as "unusually elegant and meditative," once more available with an updated afterword by the author. Golden Prague seemed mostly gray when Patricia Hampl first went there in quest of her Czech heritage. In that bleak time, no one could have predicted the political upheaval awaiting Communist Europe and the city of Kafka and Rilke. Hampl's subsequent memoir, a brilliant evocation of Czech life under socialism, attained the stature of living history, and added to our understanding not only of Central Europe but also of what it means to be engaged in the struggle of a people to define and affirm themselves. ~ from *Amazon.com*

92 50 Fantastic Life Story Quotations

For an inspirational lift or a grace note in your promotional materials you can't beat a good quotation. Over the years I've amassed a collection of quotes that relate to life stories and I'm pleased to share them with you here.

> *"Memoir writing, gathering words onto pieces of paper, helps me shape my life to a manageable size. By discovering plot, arc, theme, and metaphor, I offer my life an organization, a frame, which would be otherwise unseen, unknown. Memoir creates a narrative, a life story. Writing my life is a gift I give to myself. To write is to be constantly reborn. On one page I understand this about myself. On the next page, I understand that."* ~ from Sue William Silverman's *Fearless Confessions: A Writer's Guide to Memoir*

> *"It's not about dinner but the kind of conversations you have with your family and the stories you tell."* ~ Robyn Fivush ~ Professor of Psychology, Emory University

> *"If you want to understand today, you have to search yesterday."* ~ Pearl S. Buck – (1892-1973) American writer

"Anyone who's fortunate enough to live to be 50 years old should take some time, even if it's just a couple of weekends, to sit down and write the story of your life, even if it's only twenty pages, and even if it's only for your children and grandchildren." ~ former President Bill Clinton

"To forget one's ancestors is to be a brook without a source, a tree without a root." ~ Chinese proverb

"Do not wait; the time will never be 'just right.' Start where you stand, and work with whatever tools you may have at your command, and better tools will be found as you go along." ~ George Herbert a Welsh poet, orator and priest

"The positive thing about writing is that you connect with yourself in the deepest way, and that's heaven. You get a chance to know who you are, to know what you think. You begin to have a relationship with your mind." ~ Natalie Goldberg, writer, Zen practitioner and teacher

"When you speak or write in your own voice you become subject rather than object. You transform your own destiny." ~ bell hooks, American author, feminist and social activist

"It seems that the ancient Medicine Men understood that listening to another's story somehow gives us the strength of example to carry on, as well as showing us aspects of ourselves we can't easily see. For listening to the stories of others—not to their precautions or personal commandments—is a kind of water that breaks the fever of our isolation. If we listen closely enough, we are soothed into remembering our common name." ~ from *The Book of Awakening* by Mark Nepo

"One regret I have: I didn't get as much of the family history as I could have for the kids." ~ Robert De Niro, American actor, director, and producer

"Ultimately, the richest resource for meaning and healing is one we already possess. It rests (mostly untapped) in the material of our own life story, in the sprawling, many-layered 'text' that has been accumulating within us across the years." ~ from *Restorying Our Lives: Personal Growth through Autobiographical Reflection* by Gary M. Kenyon and William L. Randall (1997)

"Your story, it's not boring and ordinary, by the way. We just get the one life, you know. Just one. You can't live someone else's or think it's more important just because it's more dramatic. What happens matters, maybe only to us, but it matters." ~ from the movie *Ghost Town*

"If my doctor told me I had only six minutes to live, I wouldn't brood. I'd type a little faster." ~ Isaac Asimov, science fiction writer

"The best way to become acquainted with a subject is to write a book about it." ~ Benjamin Disraeli , British statesman who served twice as Prime Minister

"The longer we listen to one another—with real attention— the more commonality we will find in all our lives. That is, if we are careful to exchange with one another life stories and not simply opinions." ~ Barbara Deming, American feminist and advocate of nonviolent social change

"Do not forget the things your eyes have seen or let them slip from your heart as long as you live. Teach them to your children and your children's children." ~ Deuteronomy 4:9

"God gave us memories so that we might have roses in December." ~ James M. Barrie, Scottish novelist and dramatist, best remembered for creating Peter Pan

"It's a long time...a lifetime since I smelt those particular blooms in that particular summer yet whenever I've seen a currant bush since, wherever I was, and have lowered my face to it, the scent and pink bring the whole thing back." ~ from *I Passed This Way* by the late New Zealand writer, Sylvia Ashton-Warner

"Man is eminently a storyteller. His search for a purpose, a cause, an ideal, a mission and the like is largely a search for a plot and a pattern in the development of his life story—a story that is basically without meaning or pattern." ~ Eric Hoffer, American writer, 1902-1983

"History can be formed from permanent monuments and records; but lives can only be written from personal knowledge, which is growing every day less, and in a short time is lost forever." ~ Samuel Johnson, an English author often referred to as Dr. Johnson

"Families are united more by mutual stories—of love and pain and adventure—than by biology." ~ Daniel Taylor, from *The Healing Power of Stories*

"I think that I have been given a gift—a gift of vision. Not just the vision of photography. That is secondary to the vision that allows me to see every single life as fascinating. I honestly believe that a great novel could be written about every one of us. We all have wondrous tales written across our faces. Some are epic, some tragic, some hilarious, some elegiac, and, of course, some are spare, but I believe none would be uninteresting." ~ from *Native Soil: Photographs by Jack Spencer*

"Our stories, our personal stories, our family stories, those are our real gold. If we're lucky, as we age, we put our stories in the bank, where they gather interest in deepening meaning." ~ Richard Louv, American writer

"The best classroom in the world is at the feet of an elderly person." ~ Andy Rooney, television news commentator

"Many people wrongly assume that the most important issue among families is money and wealth transfer—it's not. What we found was the memories, the stories, the values were 10 times more important to people than the money." ~ Ken Dychtwald, American psychologist, gerontologist, documentary filmmaker, entrepreneur and best-selling author

"With the gift of listening comes the gift of healing." ~ Catherine de Hueck Doherty, a social justice worker in Canada and the United States

"Some people think we're made of flesh and blood and bones. Scientists say we're made of atoms. But I think we're made of stories. When we die, that's what people remember, the stories of our lives and the stories that we told." ~ Ruth Stotter, American storyteller

"Today, people are so disconnected that they feel they are blades of grass, but when they know who their grandparents and great-grandparents were, they become trees, they have roots, they can no longer be mowed down." ~ Maya Angelou, American poet, actress, author, and director

"The first duty of love is to listen." ~ Paul Johannes Tillich, German-American theologian and Christian existentialist philosopher

"Memories are times and places that connect our lives. I feel that lives are viewed too modestly by their owners. But lives are precious pieces of time and are as unique as fingerprints." ~ Dr. Edward Keller, American writer

"This packrat has learned that what the next generation will value most is not what we owned but the evidence of who we were and the tales of how we loved. In the end, it's the family stories that are worth the storage." ~ Ellen Goodman, *Boston Globe*

"Listening to someone talk isn't at all like listening to their words played over on a machine. What you hear when you have a face before you is never what you hear when you have before you a winding tape." ~ from *The Egotists,* by Oriana Fallaci, Italian writer, and journalist

"In all of us there is a hunger, marrow-deep, to know our heritage, to know who we are and where we came from." ~ Alex Haley, (1921 - 1992) American writer

"Like a wind crying endlessly through the universe, time carries away the names and the deeds of conquerors and commoners alike. And of all that we were, all that remains is in the memories of those who cared we came this way for a brief moment." ~ Harlan Ellison, American writer

"If you don't know your history, then you don't know anything. You are a leaf that doesn't know it is part of a tree." ~ Michael Crichton, American author, producer, director, and screenwriter

"Sing your song, dance your dance, tell your tale. ~ Frank McCourt from *Teacher Man*

"There are no ordinary lives...by stepping into the great gift of memory, we liberate ourselves." ~ Ken Burns, American documentary filmmaker

"And in that line now was a whiskered old man, with a linen cap and a crooked nose, who waited in a place called the Stardust Band Shell to share his part of the secret of heaven: that each affects the other and the other affects the next, and the world is full of stories, but the stories are all one." ~ Mitch Albom, from *The Five People You Meet in Heaven*

"If I do not connect myself with my own past...I will remain adrift from it. Those whom I have loved in the past cannot catch hold of me, for they are dead. It is I who must catch them." ~ Audre Lorde, Caribbean-American writer, poet and activist

"We are not used to associating our private lives with public events. Yet the histories of families cannot be separated from the histories of nations. To divide them is part of our denial. There are so many strands to the story... I begin to suspect each strand goes out infinitely and touches everything, everyone. I am reminded that nothing stands alone. Everything has something standing beside it. And the two are really one. A chorus of stories." ~ Susan Griffin, an American eco-feminist author

"All sorrows can be borne if you put them into a story or tell a story about them." ~ Isak Dinesen (Baroness Karen Blixen), Danish author

"To tell the story of one's life before one dies. The telling of it is an act, and for anyone whose autonomy is so often diminished, this act takes on its full importance. There is a need to give shape to one's life and to show this shape, which gives it its meaning, to someone else. Once the telling of it has been accomplished, the person seems able to let go, and to die." ~ Marie De Hennezel, French psychologist, from Intimate Death

"There is properly no history, only biography." ~ Ralph Waldo Emerson, American essayist, philosopher, and poet

"It's a pleasure to share one's memories. Everything remembered is dear, endearing, touching, precious. At least the past is safe—though we didn't know it at the time. We know it now. Because it's in the past; because we have survived." ~ Susan Sontag, author and critic, in *American Review*, New York, Sept. 1973

"I honestly believe that a great novel could be written about each and every one of us. We all have wondrous tales written across our faces. Some are epic, some tragic, some hilarious, some elegiac and, of course, some are spare—but none would be uninteresting." ~ Jack Spencer, *Readers' Digest*

"To sit alone in the lamplight with a book spread out before you and hold intimate converse with those of unseen generations—such is a pleasure beyond compare." ~ Kenko Yoshida, Japanese essayist and poet

"No man's life can be encompassed in one telling. There is no way to give each year its allotted weight, to include each event, each person who helped to shape a lifetime. What can be done is to be faithful in spirit to the record and try to find one's way to the heart of the man..." ~ John Briley, screenwriter, 1982 Academy Award winner for Best Original Screenplay, *Gandhi*

"A time's true colors fade with the passing of those who moved through it. Thus one of the oldest uses of history, oral and written, is its memorial function, the capacity to keep long-gone times vivid, recovering for those present a little of the life that might otherwise be lost." ~ James Koller's review in the *San Francisco Chronicle* (7/23/2000) of Tom Clark's book *Like It Was*

"You can make yourself live forever through writing. Do not pass through life without leaving something behind for others to learn from your experiences—even if no one but your children read it. You may discover a you you've never known." ~ Antwone Fisher, commencement address, Cleveland State University, 2003

"Life is not that which one lived, but that which one remembers, and how one remembers to tell it." ~ Gabriel Garcia Marquez, Colombian novelist, short-story writer, screenwriter and journalist

"I never thought I would write a book. I was honor-bound to dig deep and bring memories that had been suppressed for a long time, which I would have preferred to leave in the sediment of my life. But going through this process, I now feel so much better. I've forgiven people in my life, and I've forgiven myself. I feel much lighter because of it, so the process has been wonderful. I'm advising everyone I meet, all my friends, people on the street, 'Write your own book, whether you publish it or not, it feels really good.'" ~ Sting, singer & songwriter, from an interview with Katie Couric on the *Today Show* (11/4/03) regarding his autobiography, *Broken Music*

93 Why Are You a Personal Historian?

I came across this Annie Dillard quote the other day: "How we spend our days is, of course, how we spend our lives." It got me thinking.

There are times when the humdrum of keeping a personal history business afloat and tending to clients' concerns can leave me drained and questioning if this is how I want to spend my days. Why am I a personal historian? I tell myself that I'm helping families record and preserve their stories as a legacy for future generations. And I'm documenting the oral history of a particular time and place.

These are OK answers but they don't make my heart sing. They don't make me rise above the day-to-day minutiae and say, "Yes! This is how I want to spend my days!" So I dug a little deeper and I found where the gold lies.

I'm a personal historian because it aligns with four of my core values: independence, service, variety, and creativity. Let me explain. I enjoy the fact that I'm my own boss and can shape each day pretty much the way I want. I need to feel that what I do benefits others in a meaningful way. My work allows me to wear a variety of hats such as marketer, interviewer, writer, and designer. As a bonus I get to meet an amazing cross-section of people. Lastly, I love to create things. At the end of the day I can point to something I've worked on and say, "This is what I made."

When our work is aligned to our deepest values it has resonance and supports us. Sometimes I forget that in the day-to-day business of my work I need to remember where the gold lies.

Where does the gold lie for you? Why are you a personal historian?

94 A Poignant Glimpse into the Heartland of America

Thanks to my colleague Larry Lehmer at *Passing It On* for alerting me to this wonderful story.

In 1984 Peter Feldstein put up a handmade sign saying he wanted to photograph everyone in the town of Oxford, Iowa (pop. 673). He converted an abandoned storefront on Main Street into a makeshift studio. The project was a success. He captured 670 of the townsfolk.

Twenty-one years later he returned to re-photograph the same people. Some had died and some had moved away but many were still living in Oxford. This time he brought a writer who told the participants they could talk about anything in their lives so long as they told "the truth."

The result is a poignant and spellbinding book, *The Oxford Project*, which the Philadelphia Inquirer described as: ... a still-life documentary, a narrative about change. This huge, handsome book, with its gatefold photographs, its maps and memories, offers a fascinating piece of contemporary history, a treasure of social and cultural commentary.

The Oxford Project made me think how we can be far more creative with the way in which we use family photos in our life story endeavors. Like *The Oxford Project*, you could try to find two photos of the same family member taken in the same location but separated by a significant span of time. You could then arrange these photos side by side to show the passage of years. Or you might create a photo block made up of all the photos of a family member arranged from the earliest baby pictures through to their adult years.

You could also show the changes in your community by finding an early archival photo of a particular location and then taking a picture of the same view today. Putting the photos side by side will provide a dramatic visual telling of the changes that have come about. You can find some wonderful examples in the Then and Now group on Flickr.

95 How Do We Rekindle the 'Sacred' in Our Work?

Our people lived as part of everything. We were so much a part of nature, we were just like the birds, the animals, the fish. We were like the mountains. Our people lived that way. We knew there was an intelligence, a strength, a power, far beyond ourselves. We knew that everything here didn't just happen by accident. ~ David Elliott Sr. (Saltwater People, School District 63 (Saanich, 1990)

A few years ago I had the privilege of hearing First Nation elder John Elliot of the WASÁNEĆ (Saanich) territory address the 16th Annual Association of Personal Historians conference in Victoria, B.C. He spoke reverently of the stories that were passed down to him about the land and sea and animals and the values to live by.

I was moved by his dedication to his people and by the importance he places on the preserving and recording of their stories. Too often I find myself caught up in the mechanics of my work as a personal historian. There's marketing to do, blog articles to write, and deadlines to meet. I forget about the sacredness of our work. And by sacred I don't mean religious. I mean knowing someone deeply, being touched by our common humanity, and venerating the interconnectedness of all life.

What can we do to rekindle the "sacred" in our work? Here are some thoughts.

Begin with our elders.

We need to connect regularly with our own past and show reverence for our elders. This might mean ending or starting each day with some personal expression of remembrance and gratitude for family members who hold a special place in our hearts. It could mean being mindful of the elders in our community and extending a smile or helping hand.

Make time for reflection.

We need to take time out from our busyness for reflection. We need to connect to our sacred moments. Find a space where you can sit quietly and recall a sacred moment in your life. Remember what was happening and how it felt. Let that moment wash over you.

Listen for the connections.

There's a Bantu expression, Ubuntu, which translates as *I am because you are; you are because I am.* It speaks to our interconnectedness as human beings. When I'm working with clients, I'm aware that some part of their stories touches my own.

Create a personal belief statement.

We need to find a statement that gets to the heart of what we do as personal historians. It's not just words to use in a tag line but a touchstone that can remind us of why this work is sacred. Start by writing, "I am a personal historian because I believe that..." Play around with phrases until you have an "Aha!" moment. For me that moment came when I wrote, "I am a personal historian because I believe that preserving memories is an act of love." Whenever I lose my way, I try to remember that statement and why I'm doing this work.

Write it. Don't just think it.

We know how much we learn from listening to our clients' stories. But how many of us have actually told our clients this in writing? Too often I'm guilty of not taking the time to pen a thank you note that acknowledges the wisdom that I've gained from my clients.

Keep a "thank you" file.

I have a file where I keep the letters of appreciation I've received from clients and their families over the years. It also includes excerpts from personal histories that particularly touch me. When I need a pick-me-up, I go to that file and read through the collection. It reminds me of why I do this work and reconnects me to the sacred.

> *We do not believe in ourselves until someone reveals that deep inside us something is valuable, worth listening to, worthy of our trust, sacred to our touch.* ~ e. e. cummings

96 Attention Personal Historians! Don't Miss These Movies!

Get out the popcorn, turn down the lights, and settle back for a feast of "personal history" films. These movies vary in quality but are all worth viewing. They address issues that we have an interest in as personal historians. I must admit my two favorites are *Big Fish* by American director Tim Burton and *The Barbarian Invasions* by Canadian director Denys Arcand. Here are some more recommendations.

Must Read After My Death. (2008)

"While raising a family of four in 1960s Connecticut, Allis and Charley tried to repair their marriage by turning to therapy, the consequences of which are revealed in a bombshell collection of audio diaries, left to the children after Allis's death. For filmmaker Morgan Dews, what began as a simple documentary about his grandmother becomes a shocking portrait of one American family, as well as a detailed rendering of a bygone era." ~ Netflix

51 Birch Street. (2006)

"Married 54 years, Mike and Mina Block were the picture of if not wedded bliss then at least rock-solid stability—or so thought their son, documentary filmmaker Doug Block. But when his mother dies unexpectedly and his father swiftly marries his former secretary, Doug suddenly realizes there was more to his parents' union than met his eye. Turning his lens on his own family, he discovers much he never knew about the people who raised him." ~ Netflix

Uncle Nino. (2005)

"An elderly Italian peasant who barely speaks English, Uncle Nino (Pierrino Mascarino) travels to America to reconnect with nephew Robert (Joe Mantegna) and his family (played by Anne Archer, Gina Mantegna and Trevor Morgan). Trouble is, nobody communicates because they're too busy leading hectic, disconnected lives. It's up to wise Uncle Nino to bring them together and teach them what's important in life: each other. Robert Shallcross directed. " ~ Netflix

The Notebook. (2004)
"Two young lovers (Ryan Gosling and Rachel McAdams) are torn apart by war and class differences in the 1940s in this adaptation of Nicholas Sparks's best-selling novel. Their story is told by a man (James Garner) who, years later, reads from a notebook while he visits a woman in a nursing home (Gena Rowlands). Nick Cassavetes directs this heart-tugging romance about the sacrifices people will make to hang on to their one true love." ~ Netflix

The Final Cut. (2004)
"Robin Williams stars in this futuristic tale as Alan Hakman, a "cutter" who edits people's digital memories into compositions fit for viewing at their funerals—but things change when he finds his own childhood memory in the databank of a client. This thriller also stars Mira Sorvino as Hakman's girlfriend and Jim Caviezel as a former cutter who is in search of a corporate bigwig's incriminating footage." ~ Netflix

Big Fish. (2003)
"In this Tim Burton fantasy based on the novel by Daniel Wallace, William Bloom (Billy Crudup) tries to learn more about his dying father, Edward, by piecing together disparate facts from a lifetime of fantastical tales and legends of epic proportions." ~ Netflix

The Barbarian Invasions. (2003)
"When 50-something divorcé Rémy (Rémy Girard) is hospitalized for terminal cancer, his estranged son, Sébastien (Stéphane Rousseau), returns home to make amends in this Oscar-winning sequel to Denys Arcand's *Decline of the American Empire*. As Sébastien steers through the moldering health care system to bring comfort to his father, he finds

common ground with Rémy as he learns about the man through friends and lovers from his complicated past." ~ Netflix

Iris. (2001)
"Iris Murdoch (Judi Dench and Kate Winslet, in Oscar-nominated roles) was l'enfant terrible of the literary world in early 1950s Britain—a live wire who thumbed her nose at conformity via a voracious and scandalous sexual appetite. In this snippet of her life, an aging Murdoch (Dench) faces the onset of Alzheimer's disease and the loss of memories about her younger self (Winslet). Jim Broadbent won the Oscar for his portrayal of her husband." ~ Netflix

Into the Arms of Strangers. (2000)
"Filmmaker Mark Jonathan Harris's Oscar-winning documentary tells the story of an underground railroad—the Kindertransport—that saved the lives of more than 10,000 Jewish children at the dawn of World War II. Through interviews and archival footage, the survivors movingly recount being taken from their families and sent to live with strangers in the relative safety of England. Judi Dench narrates." ~ Netflix

After Life. (1999)
"At a way station somewhere between heaven and earth, the newly dead are greeted by guides. Over the next three days, they will help the dead sift through their memories to find the one defining moment of their lives. The chosen moment will be re-created on film and taken with them when the dead pass on to heaven. This grave, beautifully crafted film reveals the surprising and ambiguous consequences of human recollection." ~ Netflix

Nobody's Business. (1996)

"Director Alan Berliner takes on his reclusive father as the reluctant subject of this family documentary. Through interviews with his father, mother, sister, and other family members, Berliner examines his father's personality, family dynamics, and history." ~ Library Media Project.

My Life. (1993)

"Advertising executive Michael Keaton has it all: a beautiful, pregnant wife (Nicole Kidman), a great job, a stately house … and three months to live. Tears are jerked in this affecting drama as Keaton tries to make up for lost time and come to terms with the inevitable end of his life. Screenwriter Bruce Joel Rubin (Ghost) makes his directing debut here." ~ Netflix

Defending Your Life. (1991)

"After Daniel Miller (Albert Brooks) crashes his BMW convertible into a bus, he's transported to 'Judgment City,' where he meets the love of his life, Julia (Meryl Steep). Unfortunately, Daniel needs to defend his life on earth before he can ascend to heaven with Julia. He frantically attempts to explain the positive things he's accomplished, but soon realizes that Julia may be too good for him." ~ Netflix

On Golden Pond. (1981)

"An aging couple. Ethel and Norman Thayer (Ethel: 'I almost didn't marry you 'cause it sounded like a lisp'), spend each summer at their home on Golden Pond. They are visited by daughter Chelsea with her fiancé, where they drop off his rebellious son. The story explores their relationships, among other things the relationship that Chelsea had with her father growing up, as well as what can happen to a couple in the later years of a long marriage." ~ The Internet Movie Database

I Never Sang for My Father. (1970)
"Hackman plays a New York professor who wants a change in his life, and plans to get married to his girlfriend and move to California. His mother understands his need to get away, but warns him that moving so far away could be hard on his father. Just before the wedding, the mother dies. Hackman's sister (who has been disowned by their father for marrying a Jewish man) advises him to live his own life, and not let himself be controlled by their father." ~ The Internet Movie Database

97 How a Prehistoric Cave Painting Came to My Rescue

Some time ago I was preparing a presentation on why life stories matter for a local organization. I was struggling with where to begin until quite by accident I saw a picture of a prehistoric handprint on a cave wall.

I was transfixed. It was as if this hand was reaching across those thousands of years to touch my heart. This artist, I like to think, was saying, "Look, I existed. I was flesh and blood. I painted these scenes of wild animals. I knew the hunt. I marveled at the night sky. Do not forget me."

I knew then how to start my presentation. Our life stories matter because they are part of our DNA. We all have a desire to leave behind some record of who we are. It goes right back to our earliest ancestors.

By not recording and preserving our life stories or the stories of our loved ones we are in a sense going against our very nature.

Some people in the future want to hear from you. Don't disappoint them.

98 How Old Letters and Recovered Memories Bring Satisfaction and Hope

We lay aside letters never to read them again, and at last we destroy them out of discretion, and so disappears the most beautiful, the most immediate breath of life, irrecoverable for ourselves and for others. ~ Johann Wolfgang von Goethe

Last week I was doing some spring cleaning and came across a collection of letters I had written to my parents some forty-five years ago. At the time, I was a young man teaching in Ghana. After University I'd joined CUSO, a Canadian voluntary organization similar to the Peace Corps, and had been assigned to the West African country for two years. I'd asked my mother to keep these letters as a partial record of my experience.

Last week was the first time I'd looked at them in over four decades. As I read through these tissue thin blue aerograms, covered in tightly composed script, I was deeply affected. My younger self was speaking to me across the years not only about his wonder at this new place and culture but also about his hopes and dreams. I had written:

"I feel that I want a role in life where I can work to benefit those among us who are not so privileged. I have long given up the idea that I alone can solve world problems. But I do feel that I have something and that I can contribute a little to working out some of our problems."

In a powerful way I came to see that the life I had hoped for has been lived. The values I held then are still close to my heart. It gives me encouragement as I look ahead to the "third chapter" of my life. I suspect it will be every bit as challenging and eye-opening as my days in Ghana. And I hope I'll face the future with the same degree of passion, curiosity, dedication, and openness as that young man did all those years ago.

The letters also confirm how much detail and texture of our past is simply lost unless we have journals or letters to refresh our memory. I was surprised at the events, people, and places that had faded from my mind. In fact, it turns out that the Ghanaian secondary school compound where I lived and taught wasn't exactly how I remembered it at all!

My letters home illustrate the great value that memorabilia play in unlocking the stories of our life. But not just the stories. Those letters also helped me understand something of the person I am today.

Here are a few random thoughts:

- *Start a journal.* It's never too late. Begin recording the details of your life. One day you may want to write your life story and these journal entries will be invaluable.

- *Preserve old letters.* Make sure that you keep your correspondence safely stored in acid free archival boxes.

- *Search for original documents.* If you've been hired to produce a personal history or you're doing your own, make sure to uncover any letters, journals, or photographs that will help trigger memories.

- *Use archival documents to reveal values and beliefs.* While memorabilia can aid in triggering a recall of past events, go further. The stories that emerge from the past can provide powerful clues to the essence of a person and the things that person holds dear.

99 It's Time to Honor Our Elders

The other day in Zoomer magazine I read an interview with the English actress Emma Thompson. When asked what made her unhappy, she said:

> *That, much to our great loss, we've turned away from the notion of elders, of wisdom. It's an absolute disaster for the old and the young. It leads to fractures everywhere. But mostly a fracture in our concept of what it is to be human.*

I'm reminded that in recording and preserving an older person's life story we are engaged in important work. We are honoring an elder. We are saying to that person, you count. Your life holds lessons for me and for future generations. I value your story and don't want it lost.

What a wonderful difference it would make in our communities if all our older citizens had the opportunity to tell their story. We would indeed become a more humane society. What are you doing to capture an elder's life story?

Here are four books that demonstrate the wisdom and spirit of older people.

- *In the Arms of Elders: A Parable of Wise Leadership and Community Building* (Paperback) by William H. Thomas
- *What Are Old People For? How Elders Will Save the World* (Paperback) by William H. Thomas
- *Number Our Days* (Paperback) by Barbara Myerhoff
- *How to Live: A Search for Wisdom from Old People (While They Are Still on This Earth)* (Hardcover) by Henry Alford

100 Remember When. Songs That Recall Our Yesterdays

Music can evoke strong feelings and memories. It's one of the ways we personal historians can help clients unlock stories from their past.

Not long ago some of my colleagues in the Association of Personal Historians began compiling a list of their favorite songs that brought back memories. I've included some of them here and added some of my own. To listen to these selections, just click on the title.

Here are three songs that resonate with me:

- *Time in a Bottle* performed by Jim Croce

"If I could save time in a bottle/The first thing that I'd like to do/Is to save every day 'til eternity passes away/Just to spend them with you"

- *The Way We Were* performed by Barbra Streisand

"Memories, may be beautiful and yet/what's too painful to remember/we simply choose to forget/So it's the laughter we will remember/whenever we remember/the way we were."

- *In My Life* performed by Allison Crowe

"There are places I remember/All my life though some have changed/Some forever not for better/Some have gone and some remain/All these places have their moments"

Here are some other great songs from my friends at the APH. What are the songs that speak to you about the past?

- *Time of Your Life* performed by Green Day

"It's not a question/but a lesson learned in time./It's something unpredictable but in the end it's right./ I hope you had the time of your life./ So take the photographs and still frames in your mind."

- *Grandpa (Tell Me 'Bout the Good Old Days)* performed by the Judds

"Grandpa, tell me bout the good old days/Sometimes it feels like this world's gone crazy/And Grandpa, take me back to yesterday"

- *Remember When* performed by Alan Jackson

"Remember when thirty seemed so old/Now lookin' back it's just a steppin' stone/To where we are,/Where we've been/Said we'd do it all again/Remember when/Remember when we said when we turned gray/When the children grow up and move away/We won't be sad, we'll be glad/For all the life we've had/And we'll remember when"

• *My Best Days Are Ahead of Me* performed by Danny Gokey

"Blowing out the candles/on another birthday cake/Old enough to look back and laugh at my mistakes/Young enough to look at the future and like what I see/My best days are ahead of me"

• *Old Friends/Bookends* performed by Simon & Garfunkel

"Time it was, and what a time it was, it was/A time of innocence, a time of confidences/Long ago, it must be, I have a photograph/Preserve your memories, they're all that's left you."

• *Those Were the Days, My Friends* performed by Mary Hopkins

"Once upon a time there was a tavern/Where we used to raise a glass or two/Remember how we laughed away the hours/And think of all the great things we would do"

• *As Time Goes By* performed by Frank Sinatra

"You must remember this/A kiss is just a kiss, a sigh is just a sigh./The fundamental things apply/As time goes by."

101 6 Ways to Rekindle the Passion in Your Freelance Work

The other day I was having coffee with a colleague and she asked me how I kept my "saw sharp." Good question. No matter how much we love our work, the day-to-day demands can eventually wear us down and make us dull.

I've been self-employed for over three decades and know what it's like to lose my spark. Here are some ways I've found to get it back. Maybe they'll work for you.

1. Connection

Working solo can be an isolating experience. Being able to meet with colleagues is a great tonic. I get energized meeting locally with fellow personal historians. As well, being connected online through my membership in the Association of Personal Historians is a wonderful source of support and information. Make sure you've got a support group that can give you an added boost when your spirits are low.

2. Variety

I admit that I get bored doing the same thing over and over again. Knowing this means I look for ways to build variety into my work.

I started a blog in part because I wanted to try something new. I've also expanded my repertoire beyond video productions to include print and audio projects.

Look for ways that you can add some new pieces to the work you do.

3. Continuous learning

I'm a perpetual student. I love to learn new things. Besides books, there are online workshops and courses that keep me up-to-date and fresh.

Another super way to keep learning is going to a professional conference. I've attended two Association of Personal Historians conferences. These are jam-packed with workshops and talks. Each time I go, I come away feeling revitalized.

Plan to attend one professional conference this year. You won't regret it.

4. Time out

No matter how much you love your work, if you never take a break from it, you run the real risk of losing your spark.

For this reason I've built into my days and weeks "play time." Whether it's meditating, going for a walk, visiting with friends, or just goofing off, I get away from my work.

What kind of play time have you built into your work week?

5. Inspiration

I find that being around positive, inspiring people and reading or listening to inspiring stories does a lot to rekindle my enthusiasm.

I know I'm not alone. Over 15 million YouTube viewers have watched *Randy Pausch Last Lecture: Achieving Your Childhood Dreams.*

Take the time to find inspiring stories that will recharge your batteries.

6. Acknowledgment

When I'm feeling flat and uninspired, I sometimes go to my "Thank You" folder. Here I keep all of the notes and letters sent to me by satisfied and grateful clients.

Reading through these brings a smile to my face and a reminder of why I love my work.

Make sure to put all your support letters in a file where you can find them. And periodically take them out and read them.

102 No One Dies Wishing They Had More Shoes

Spending money on things will not make us as happy as spending on experiences.

This is the conclusion of recent study conducted by Ryan Howell, an assistant professor of psychology at San Francisco State University.

According to SFU's press release, the study, "demonstrates that experiential purchases, such as a meal out or theater tickets, result in increased well-being because they satisfy higher order needs, specifically the need for social connectedness and vitality—a feeling of being alive." Professor Howell explained in an interview:

> *Purchased experiences provide memory capital. We don't tend to get bored of happy memories like we do with a material object...it's not that material things don't bring any happiness. It's just that they don't bring as much...You're happy with a new television set. But you're thrilled with a vacation.*

This study got me thinking. It brought to mind some of the great experiences in my life—being a volunteer teacher in Ghana for two years, snorkeling over a coral reef in Tobago, meeting my partner 41 years ago and volunteering at Victoria Hospice every Tuesday morning.

I was particularly struck by the study's link between long-term happiness and social connectedness. For me, this again speaks to the importance of helping people record and preserve their life stories.

Whether we're sitting down with a family member, friend or neighbor, we are not just collecting stories. We are connecting with people and in the process bringing a little happiness into the world.

What are some of your great life experiences?

Acknowledgments

THIS BOOK WOULD NOT have been possible without the help of the following people: first and foremost Jim Osborne, my life partner and writing mentor who painstakingly copyedited every post in my original blog; Kathleen McGreevy at Chapter Savers who did a great job as editor, categorizing and arranging all of my blog posts into a coherent book; Monica Lee at Clickago Storywerks who formatted the ebook and paperback and designed an eye-catching cover; Sarah White, APH President, and the APH Board, who approached me with the idea of converting my blog posts into a book; Linda Coffin, APH Executive Director, who carefully shepherded the project along; and all my regular blog readers who encouraged me and made it a delight to write for them. Thank you.

About the Author

DAN CURTIS IS AN award-winning documentary filmmaker, writer, certified life coach, and professional personal historian. He lives in Victoria, British Columbia.

If you enjoyed this book, please consider leaving a review at Amazon, even it's only a line or two. It helps get the word out about the profession of Personal Historians and would be very much appreciated.

Sample of
Business Tips for Personal Historians

WANT MORE IDEAS? COMING May 2015: Author Dan Curtis also wrote *Business Tips for Personal Historians: 92 Lessons Learned from a Veteran Storyteller,* filled with suggestions and lessons drawn from his years of experience in the field of helping others tell their life stories. Here's a sample:

3 Big Start-Up Mistakes I Made That You Can Avoid

Thinking of giving up your current job and starting up your own business? Here are a few big mistakes I made and lessons I learned. Maybe they'll save you some anguish. Then again maybe you're smarter than I was. ;-)

In 1980 I left my job at TVOntario, an educational broadcaster, and hung up my shingle as an independent documentary filmmaker. I had a passion for documentaries, a willingness to work hard, and a creative bent. What I didn't have was two cents in my bank account. That was my first mistake.

The early years were tough. I had to borrow money from friends and get odd jobs to pay the rent and buy groceries. The effort expended on survival left little time or energy for filmmaking. Eventually I went on to be a successful documentary filmmaker but it was a lesson well learned.

Lesson 1: Don't start without money in the bank. You'll need enough cash in hand to cover at least a year of living and business expenses. The first couple of years will be lean.

My next big mistake.

Although I was enthusiastic, I had no documentary film experience and no body of work. Few were willing to take on an eager but inexperienced filmmaker.

Lesson 2: Gain experience and have something to show potential clients. Enthusiasm is important but clients also want to know that you can deliver. If you have little experience, highlight aspects from your previous work that indicate you can do the job.

For example, I drew on the fact that I had a Masters of Education degree. As part of that degree I had taken a course in the production and evaluation of educational media and had made a short animated film. I pointed to my work at TVOntario as a producer and as a writer of educational materials. It was a stretch but it illustrated that I was competent and had some "media" experience even if I hadn't made a documentary.

Mistake number three.

I launched into my new business with no plan, no advice, and no clear idea of what was involved in being an independent documentary filmmaker. Not something I'd recommend to others. Had I known what to expect, it could have saved me from a good deal of heartache.

Lesson 3: Have a plan. Seek advice. Know what you're getting into. You don't need to turn this into a year-long research and development project. But tempering your enthusiasm with a little dose of reality will serve you well. Trust me!

WANT TO LEARN MORE tips like this?

Get *Business Tips for Personal Historians:*
92 Lessons Learned from a Veteran Storyteller

available from the Association of Personal Historians store:
http://store.personalhistorians.org/
and at major booksellers.

Made in the USA
Middletown, DE
03 June 2017